Paste, Pencils, Scissors
and   Crayons

Paste, Pencils, Scissors and Crayons

Gene Baer

Parker Publishing Company, Inc.   West Nyack, New York

Library of Congress Cataloging in Publication Data

Baer, Gene
   Paste, pencils, scissors, and crayons.

   Includes index.
   1. Creative activities and seat work. I. Title.
LB1537.B23   372.5   79-9911
ISBN 0-13-652776-0

Printed in the United States of America.

To

GRETCHEN

A Word from the Author

Nearly everything in this book can be made *quickly and easily* out of paper with paste, pencils, scissors and crayons. Although some of these lessons would profit from the use of staplers, markers, and other specialized art supplies, few actually require their use.

One of the great advantages in working with paste, pencils, scissors and crayons is that these materials are within reach of all schools and most homes. Once the children in your class have discovered the unlimited joys of creating with these simple materials, they will also have learned that creativity is a state of mind—that one does not need expensive craft kits, elaborate paint sets, or basement pottery kilns to put strong wings to thought. Children who can create with paste, pencils, scissors and crayons are obviously happy children, for they are kids who are never at a loss for ways in which to spend their time productively.

Paste, Pencils, Scissors and Crayons is a carefully presented series of lesson plans that have been thoroughly classroom-tested. Working with all types of kids, I eliminated those plans that didn't work and kept those that did, tooling each lesson to an extremely high degree of teaching readiness. The lessons in this book are the survivors of innumerable attempts on my part over many years to arrive at a high-quality set of art lessons which can be taught year after year with success.

Most of the arts and crafts lessons in this book grew out of my own experimentation. Those that did not are either "classics" in their field, or are lessons of great potential that for one reason or another have never received the popularity that they deserve. All of these lessons have endured because they work.

These lessons teach children valuable concepts of using lines and colors, concepts of design and structure and perception, about working with tools and completing what they start. They teach these effectively because the children enjoy what they are doing.

For example, one of the most effective lessons, particularly with kindergartners, is the "Picnic Lunch" project. Why does this extremely simple lesson succeed time after time where more ambitious lesson plans have failed? I don't know. I can only tell you that this well-tested lesson hits little children with all the emotional impact of an explosion.

You'll find that the "Holidays and Festivals" section will be unusually helpful. For instance, the three Halloween lessons are each distinctly different, but all of them provide quality learning material. And at Christmas time—if your class has half the fun that mine have had with the Christmas Snake—I can unequivocally guarantee you a joyful Christmas!

If at another time of year you need something special to overcome classroom boredom, turn to Chapter Seven. If there is anything a kid loves it's a picture that *does* something. Any art project that flips, flops, talks, winks, peeks, barks, sings, or flies has to be a classroom prizewinner!

Your time will be well spent reading the first three chapters thoroughly before you flip through the main body of *Paste, Pencils, Scissors and Crayons* in search of treasures. Naturally certain chapters will be more valuable to you than others, but, regardless of the age level of the children with whom you meet, don't pass over the chapter entitled "Starting With The Very Young." There are valuable tips, tricks, advice and suggestions here helpful for teaching all ages. In fact, you'll find something helpful to you in every chapter, on every page.

So whether you are an inexperienced teacher who needs help and direction in presenting an art lesson, or an experienced teacher who is still searching for "something new," or even a fellow art teacher who recognizes a worthwhile art lesson when one comes along—*Paste, Pencils, Scissors and Crayons* is addressed to you and your needs.

Contents

9

Paste, Pencils, Scissors and Crayons

1

"Hey, Teacher"!

Every good how-to-do-it book begins with a *general* introduction—but this particular chapter also contains a lot of *specific* information that is not found elsewhere; so begin at the beginning and I promise you that your time will be well spent!

lesson 1   **You Mean That
You're a Teacher
and You Can't
Draw?**

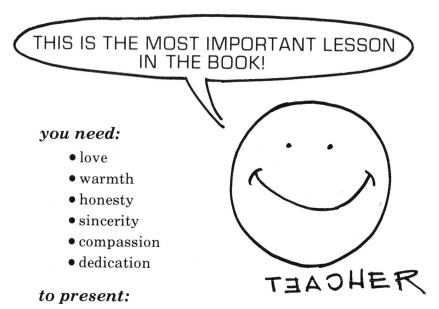

you need:
- love
- warmth
- honesty
- sincerity
- compassion
- dedication

to present:

So you can't draw? That's the best news I've heard all day! If I were a little kid in your class and I found out that I could draw better than my teacher, what an incentive *that* would be for me to spread my wings and try to fly a little higher! I don't want to hurt your feelings, but the truth is that nobody in your class cares if you can draw or not!

This isn't a drawing book. Believe it or not, there isn't a single lesson here that will make you wheel your inadequacies out into the limelight. So whether you draw like an angel or scratch like a chicken, your secret is safe with me. As far as I'm concerned, *how you draw* is a personal matter that goes far beyond the scope of this book; but *how you teach*—THAT is very important!

I have been a teacher for a good many years and I am still overawed by the number of "failures" who manage to succeed and by the obvious talent that fails, so a good teacher *has* to be one who instills in his kids a solid belief that *all things are possible to those who continue to try.*

And speaking of trying, how about you? If your drawing ability is less than you would like it to be, don't let this evaluation cripple you. So what if there are those in your class who can draw better than you? There is no shame in being less than others, but please, whatever you do, DON'T disparage your own abilities, for if you belittle yourself, what will happen to that little kid whose talents may be *less* than yours? Remember, you're the ambassador of trying. Live by it!

And if you're asked, "Can you draw?" say "Yes— maybe not as well as you, but with practice I'm getting better every day!" And after you have said it, try to believe it.

For that's what education is all about.

TEACHƎЯ
1-1

lesson 2   **You!**

The lessons in this book are as easy to present as any lessons that you will ever find anywhere. Each is expressly designed for the teacher who has little or no art background. They're written for *you!*

you need:

- warmth
- enthusiasm
- an appreciation for art
- and the understanding that there are different ways of seeing

to present:

The Essential Ingredient

Just because the lessons in this book are easy to present, it does not mean that you get time off, for the success or failure of any lesson depends to a great extent upon how well you can present your material, how much continued enthusiasm you can engender, and the love with which you reward the finished results.

Some of your kids need constant encouragement, some need time just to create, others need the acceptance that they do not get at home—in one way or another, they all need *you*!

Ways of Seeing

To study art is to develop an appreciation for other ways of seeing. The moment one realizes that not only *the way* in which we see pictures, but even the *very ability* to see pictures as pictures is a skill that is culturally acquired, one becomes less bigoted in the appreciation of other ways of seeing. Just because we do not always understand cave pictures, African masks, Islamic miniatures, or Oriental scrolls, it does not mean that any of these other-culture artists are in any way stupid or inferior people. Different? Yes. Stupid? Don't count on it! This also applies to those two little kids who sit in the back of the room, and to child art in general.

For example: a thoughtless adult will sometimes chide a child for making this drawing of a house. (See Figure 1-2.)

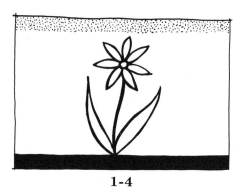

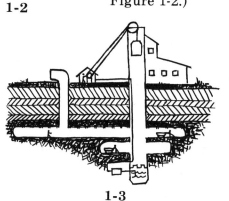

1-2

1-3   1-4

And yet, moments later this same adult might illustrate a point by drawing this diagram of a coal mine on a classroom chalkboard. Is there really a difference? (See Figure 1-3.)

The girl who draws this picture of a flower is not stupid either. She knows exactly what she is doing. The top streak is the sky, the bottom streak is the grass, and the space in the middle? Why, that's the air! (See Figure 1-4.)

If you were to ask this child why she didn't color the sky "down to the ground," she will look at you strangely.

She knows that the sky doesn't touch the ground, whether her teacher knows it or not! And that's the way she draws it.

Final Thoughts

We should all be encouraged to develop an appreciation for other ways of seeing. This means that we are obligated to teach children about ways of seeing other than their own—after all, we don't want *them* to grow up to be intolerant!

lesson 3   **Teaching an Art Lesson**

you need:

- a warm classroom climate
- a leisurely presentation
- and more than a dash of showmanship

to present:

As any experienced teacher knows, the proper presentation makes all the difference. Good lesson plans can be bungled in many ways: perhaps the following paragraphs can lead you through some of the more obvious pitfalls.

Be Familiar with Your Material. If time permits, become familiar with your material by doing it first yourself; if you are rushed for time, take at least a few minutes to figure out the basic steps so that the lesson can be presented without stumbling.

Your Delivery. Speak clearly and take your time! Try to present your material with as much showmanship as you can muster.

Keep all Procedural Steps as Simple as Possible. The temptation is to explain too much at one time, whereas the bald truth is that it is practically impossible to make your procedural steps too small!

Don't Assume too Much. For example:

1. When working with complex cutting instructions, have the kids *scribble* in the areas to be removed. This way, there is no mistaking the paper to be cut away!

2. If something has an important top and bottom, don't put too much faith in your verbal instructions. Have the kids pencil a "T" at the top and *then* proceed!

3. Talk *their* language. Words like "widthwise" and "lengthwise" are not common childhood words, so instead of using sentences like, "Fold the paper lengthwise," the kids will respond much better to something like, "Fold the paper to make a skinny book."

Collect the Completed Work. Children who come from homes in which their art is appreciated will want to take their art home. Others want desperately to give their drawings to somebody who cares. *Be that somebody.* Even if you know that you don't have the time to display all the finished products, ask for them. It is your job to do for these kids what their parents cannot.

Display, Display, Display...Whenever possible, hang their work all around the room. Make it a happy place to live in and let this happiness spill out into the halls and stairways. Art is meant to be seen. That's what it's all about.

lesson 4   **Materials**

When I first started to write this book, I had planned to limit my materials to paper, paste, pencils, scissors and crayons, but as the book began to take shape I realized

that it would be foolish to assume that the average reader did not have access to other tools and materials such as staplers, markers, etc. Therefore, although most everything in this book *can* be made with paste, pencils, scissors and crayons, I have made no great effort to avoid the use of other specialized tools and materials. In fact, in many places I will be the first to recommend their use!

Paper

Paper comes in a variety of different styles, sizes, weights, and surfaces. The most common of these are listed below:

1. *Drawing Papers.* The three most common school drawing papers are newsprint, manila drawing paper, and white drawing paper. *Newsprint* is the cheapest but it is also the most fragile. *Manila drawing paper* has more body to it but it is cream-colored. *White drawing paper* is the best but it is also the most expensive.

2. *Colored Paper.* Although there are many kinds of colored papers, the most common is called *construction* paper. It is stiff enough to be fun to fold, heavy enough to take limited abuse, and of course comes in dozens of different colors. However, it is not lightproof. If for any reason you need a light-resistant construction paper, you'll have to order it and pay the difference!

3. *Lightweight White 8½ x 11" Papers.* For these no special purchase is required, for every school that I have ever visited has an abundance of duplicating and mimeograph papers. Both of these papers are fun to draw on and this size and weight of paper plays an important role in many of the lessons found in this book.

4. *Tagboard.* Tagboard is a stiff, lightweight, cream-colored cardboard that is perfect for pattern-making, etc.

Paste and Glue

Paste. Here, you get what you pay for. Although it is possible to buy some brands for as much as one-third the cost of others, the cheaper brands often just contain more water. So what you save in money you might also gain in frustration!

If you are low on paste, your class might welcome the opportunity to make their own. If you have never done it, the recipe is fantastically simple. Just add flour and water together until it acts like paste. Once you have done it, you become an instant authority!

Glue. The best classroom glue is called *white glue* and it is sold under a variety of brand names. While wet it is white and opaque but it dries to a clear film. Also, it can be thinned with water. White glue is sold in all sizes of plastic squeeze bottles, some as small as 1¼ ounces. When it comes to giving a permanent bond, glue is superior to paste. It is also about twice as expensive!

Scissors

Here again, you get what you pay for. Inexpensive scissors cut, but more expensive scissors cut better. Scissors are sold in three classroom styles; pointed, semi-pointed, and blunt.

Although generations of adults have warned against the dangers of pointed and semi-pointed scissors, and many cautious school administrators have legislated against their use, I personally have never known of any accidents that could be blamed on these scissors. This does not mean that accidents haven't happened or that children should not be warned about the inherent evil in sharp points, but with children—say, eight years or older—I question if the case against possible injury is strong enough to outlaw their supervised use.

Decorating Materials

Crayons. All standard brands of crayons are good. Although many authorities recommend the kindergarten size for a wide range of children, kids do not always agree with the text books. In my experience, most kids of seven or older—if given a choice—will choose the smaller standard-size crayons.

The larger kindergarten-size crayons are sold in *tuck* and in *lift-lid* boxes. What's the difference? Price! Although the lift-lid boxes are more durable, you are going to pay more. You can also buy crayons in a hinged metal box—and for this you can expect to pay nearly twice as much!

Crayons are sold in two basic shapes, cylindrical and anti-roll (flat on one side). I'm not sure that I can recommend one over the other. The anti-roll may not roll but in my experience they break more easily.

Markers. All markers are fun to use, but I would recommend the *watercolor* markers over the *permanent* markers. The permanent markers will not only bleed through the paper, but on some occasions will even bleed through several sheets of paper!

Markers can also be bought in a variety of points. If you can afford them, buy the fine lines as well as the broader nibs.

lesson 5 **Organizing the Mess**

Wherever there's kids there's bound to be a mess. No amount of organization will ever totally eliminate confusion, but a few pointers might help.

you need:

- patience
- a sense of humor
- leather lungs
- and a "I'll-kill-you-if-you-don't" look

to present:

Paste or Glue?

Since both paste and white glue have shortcomings as well as merits, let me give you a brief description of each:

Paste. Paste is relatively inexpensive, can be manufactured as needed, and is perfectly satisfactory for most paper projects. On the negative side, it doesn't hold as well as white glue, has been known to play host to a green mold, and some children eat it!

White Glue. If you want something to stay stuck, use white glue. It is easy to apply and since it has great holding power, a small amount goes a long way. It is perfect for collages, mounting pictures, and when thinned with water is used for transparent tissue designs. On the negative side, it is about twice the price of paste, the tops of the applicator squeeze bottles have a way of becoming clogged, and kids soon discover that white glue poured all over the back of the hand and allowed to dry makes "skin." (See Figure 1-5.)

1-5

Paste Management. In classrooms where children always work in small groups, many teachers like to keep paste in small wide-mouthed plastic containers with snap-on tops (margarine containers, etc., are ideal). For larger groups, it makes sense to give a pint jar to each group. If the paste level is too low to be reached by fingers, spoon a generous amount onto the inside of the jar cover—this makes as convenient a dispenser as any!

For individual work, paste pads are preferred by most teachers. A jar of paste, an old ruler, and a packet of torn scrap paper will serve nicely.

Glue Management. For most classroom projects, the small 1¼ ounce squeeze bottles are ideal. For smaller projects, put a dab of glue on a piece of paper and use a toothpick for an applicator.

Standard Sizes

Like most experienced hands, I believe in making my preparations as simple as possible, and one of the easiest places to begin with is paper size.

Paper size. Since drawing and construction papers come in standard sizes (9 x 12", 12 x 18", 18 x 24"), most of the lessons in this book begin with these sizes in mind. If smaller pieces are needed, I try to use sizes that leave usable remainders. Generally this means that smaller sheets are simply larger sheets cut in half—hence the frequent use in this book of 6 x 9" (one half 9 x 12"), 6 x 4½" (one half 6 x 9") etc.

Circle Sizes. From time to time I will refer to 3½" (watercup-size) circle patterns, and by this I mean circles the size of inverted watercups. If your classroom doesn't have access to these practical circle patterns, a usable substitute can be made from tag board.

Clean Up

Salvage. Since it makes sense to save, salvage should be an integral part of the "clean-up time." For this purpose, cardboard scrap boxes are ideal. Begin by keeping one for odds and ends of construction paper and another for broken and strayed crayons. Add other boxes as needed.

Clean-up Management. Perhaps the most efficient means of classroom management is the use of the *clean-up committee.* Post a chart indicating the make-up of each committee and the dates on which the members are responsible for keeping the room clean.

Some things, like brushes, are best cleaned by one person. When the issue is critical (such as cleaning acrylic paint from the bristles), I am sometimes happier doing it myself or giving the duty to a volunteer whose work I can check! This way I *know* I'll have brushes tomorrow.

lesson 8 ## Race, Creed, Et Cetera

Race, creed, and color are as much a part of the contemporary curriculum as the three R's were to the classrooms of the past. Judged by reasonably high standards, public education may never produce a society free from prejudice, but then again it has never given us a society that has achieved total literacy. But we keep trying.

Holidays. As much as we often try to hide it, even from ourselves, we live in a Christian culture. Christmas commemorates the birth of Christ, and Easter is His Resurrection. As teachers, however, our directive is clear. We have been given the role of de-emphasizing the Christian nature of these holidays and, if we are to celebrate them at all, they are to be secular celebrations.

But from a child's point of view, Christmas, Easter, Thanksgiving, etc., are *holidays* and as such they have a meaning that transcends the teapot squabbles that adults sometimes bring to this issue. As long as Santa Clauses, Easter Bunnies, and Pilgrims satisfy the need to give imagery to celebrations, there is no need to turn holidays into what could easily become "colorless celebrations for days appointed by law for the suspension of business in commemoration of non-events!"

So long as you allow for the recognition of individual needs and differences, there is no reason why theological differences have to become a central issue on these most festive days of the year. With sensitive leadership, this matter can be handled with ease. At Christmas time, for example, greeting cards are equally festive whether they feature menorahs, creches, or snowmen. Think of all your holidays as celebrations honoring childhood, and your fears of offending will disappear by the powers invested in children to turn any holiday into a festive celebration.

Skin Color. "White" or "Black," most of us go through life with a distorted conception as to the degree of lightness to our skins if we are white or to the degree of darkness if we are black. That the truth lies somewhere in between is best illustrated in a little classroom exercise in color selection that can be used for bridging this difference. If you are like most of the people I have shown this to, you will find this lesson as enlightening as it is amusing.

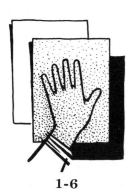

1-6

For those lessons that call for "skin-toned" construction paper I prepare a selection of papers ranging in color from peach to tan to darker shades of brown. But before I bring attention to this pile of skin paper, I give a short presentation that you can easily revise to fit your needs. My presentation goes something like this:

"The only people in this world who are white are either ghosts or clowns who have painted their faces. Nobody's white!" At this point I hold up a piece of white paper and display it against the back of my hand as I say, "Look at this sheet of paper and then look at my hand. Look at how white the paper is and how much darker my hand is. I don't know *what* color I am, but I'm certainly not white." At that point, I go about the room holding my white paper against the hands and arms of kids in various parts of the room as I repeatedly underline my theme that "Nobody's white."

I continue with, "You just can't go into an art store and ask for 'skin' paper because that's one color they don't sell. Do you know why? It's because everyone's skin is different." At this point I display all the preselected "skin" papers as I explain, "This morning I went through all of the school's construction paper supplies, and here are the closest colors that I could find to what could be called 'skin color.' You will have to decide which one is the closest to *your* skin color. So when I call you up to take a look, place your hand next to each pile and choose the color that is closest to your skin tone."

Like the old nursery tale of the *Emperor's New Clothes,* this lesson is a refreshing exposure to the unbridled honesty of children, and the younger the child the more open will be the response. Here—after a great deal of contemplation—a great many children, both "white" and "black," will choose the same shade of tan!

Each time that I give this lesson I find myself wishing that everyone could witness the solemnity of this decision-making process and the finality with which this choice is made. It's beautiful!

And then, of course, there is the inevitable question of, "What color do you *color* skin?"* To answer this question, I often have my kids play another game of color selection. This one is played with crayons.

My presentation begins in much the same way as it did in the previous exercise, only this time I have the children make color swatches and then compare the back of their hand to their crayoned scrap of paper.

I don't know about you, but for skin color I prefer a mixture of light red and light brown crayon. But that's me. You'll have to make your own comparison tests.

---

*In yesteryear the standard answer was "light orange," and pumpkin-colored people prevailed.

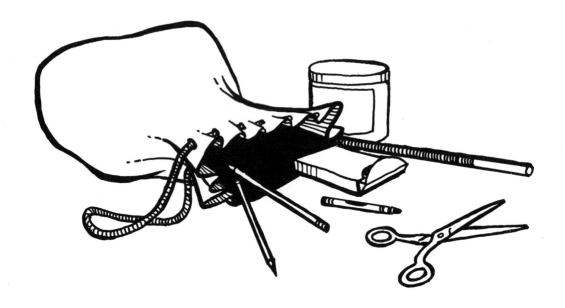

2

Your Basic Bag of Tricks

For frequently used instructions, it makes sense to give the directions once and to put all of these popular instructions under one chapter heading. This plan of presentation certainly beats repeating the same material over and over again, but it also makes for very dull reading. Therefore, I have tempered efficiency with fun by accompanying each set of directions with a lively referral lesson.

concept

lesson 1 **The Sixteen-Part Box**

I don't know of any set of instructions that has more practical applications than this box fold. In one form or another I use this basic box to make everything from cribs to Columbus boats!

you need:

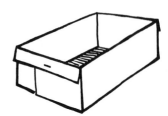

- • a rectangular sheet of paper
- • scissors
- • stapler, paste, or glue

to present:

1. Fold the paper in half widthwise. Open it up and fold the short sides to the middle. (See Figure 2-1.)

2. Repeat lengthwise the same series of folds. When you are finished your paper should have sixteen equal parts. Or, as some of your kids will tell you, *thirty-two* if you count both sides! (See Figure 2-2.)

3. Cut on the heavy lines. (See Figure 2-3.)

4. Fold up the central end-flaps first before turning in the corner flaps. (See Figure 2-4.)

5. For most, but not all, box-based constructions, turn the extending flaps over and down. Paste, staple, or glue whenever you're ready. (See Figure 2-5.)

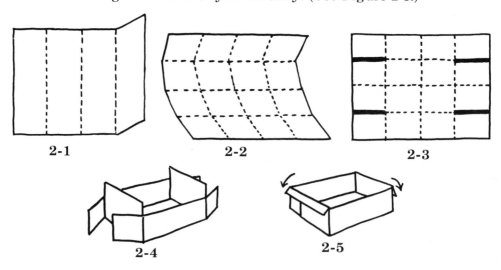

2-1   2-2   2-3

2-4   2-5

referral
lesson 1   **Easter Basket**

Little children especially love to make Easter baskets
and to fill them with "grass" and paper eggs. The box fold
is a natural for baskets!

you need:

- 12 x 18″ construction paper
- 3 x 18″ construction paper
- green "grass" paper
- white "egg" paper
- scissors and decorating materials
- stapler, paste or glue

to present

1. Using the 12 x 18″ paper, have your class make a
Sixteen-Part Box (see preceding page).
2. Fold the 2 x 18″ strip lengthwise (for strength) and
staple as shown to make a handle.
3. Cut the green paper into "grass" strips. Have your
kids crinkle these strips in their hands and then use this
grass to fill their baskets.
4. Use the white paper to draw and decorate eggs.
Have the kids cut out their eggs and place them in their
finished baskets.

Further Suggestions: For a more elaborate project,
suggest to your kids that they *decorate* these baskets. You
might also pass out brown paper for making chocolate
bunnies and small pieces of colored paper for making jelly
beans!

concept
lesson 2   **The Mystery of
Cut-Paper
Symmetry**

A child approaching a simple concept for the first
time does so with the same sense of marvel and
befuddlement that an adult experiences trying to
comprehend the latest in scientific theories. You may not

remember all the concept problems that you faced as a child, but chances are that this lesson caused its share of childhood puzzlement!

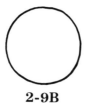

you need:

- paper
- pencils
- crayons

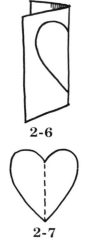

2-6

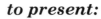

2-7

2-8

2-9A

to present:

Many young children find simple folded-paper work as hard to learn as a complicated lesson in grammar. In this and in the following lesson I'll point out some of the more obvious problems. For example:

A quick and easy way to make a heart is to draw half a heart on a folded piece of paper as shown in Figure 2-6...

When you cut out this heart it should look like Figure 2-7 ...

But if I had a nickle for every classroom broken heart that looked like Figure 2-8 ...

... I would be a wealthy man!

The secret, of course, is simply to draw the half heart touching the *fold* rather than touching the outer edge—but that isn't as much a rule to be learned as it is a concept to be understood. And for some kids that just takes time!

A good way to present this lesson is for you to make a series of cut-paper demonstrations. Perhaps you could begin by drawing a half circle against the fold of a piece of paper as in Figure 2-9A. I always make a great show out of this demonstration. Like a magician performing a trick, I carefully cut it out, open it up, and with a dramatic flair I produce "both" circles: (1) the cut paper circle, and

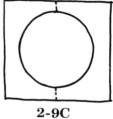

2-9B   **2-9C**

(2) the paper remainder with the circular hole cut in the middle. (See Figures 2-9B and 2-9C.)

Then, to show how easy it is to make a mistake, I repeat the process with another sheet of paper but this time I draw the half circle so that it touches the outside edge of the folded paper as in Figure 2-10A. Naturally this experiment is a failure. (See Figures 2-10B and 2-10C.) If you greet this failure with a wry face, the results will be viewed with a great deal of laughter, particularly on the part of young children.

Once the basic concept has been introduced, your kids can experiment to their heart's content. In the following lesson I'll explain a few more of the pitfalls awaiting you the day your class begins its first full-length lesson in cut-paper symmetry.

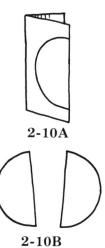

2-10A

2-10B

2-10C

referral
lesson 2 **Symmetry Greeting Cards**

In recent years a great deal of pressure has been brought to bear upon the public schools to secularize the celebration of Christian holidays. (When was the last time that you saw a schoolyard creche?) In keeping with this practice, many classes no longer make *Christmas* cards, they make *greeting* cards. If only all problems could be solved this easily!

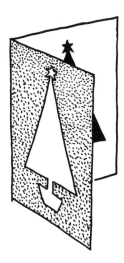

you need:

- 6 x 4½" red and green construction paper
- 6 x 9" white drawing or construction paper
- pencil, scissors, paste or glue

to present:

1. Review with your class the material on the preceding page and then demonstrate the following bugaboos that await them:

Figure 2-11A is an evergreen tree drawn correctly with the trunk on the fold.

2-11A

Figure 2-11B is what happens if the trunk is not drawn on the fold.

2-11B

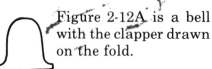
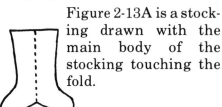

Figure 2-12A is a bell with the clapper drawn on the fold.

2-12A

Figure 2-12B is what happens if the clapper is not drawn on the fold.

2-12B

Figure 2-13A is a stocking drawn with the main body of the stocking touching the fold.

2-13A

Figure 2-13B is the same stocking with the toe touching the fold.

2-13B

Since—either way—the stocking is a failure, folded paper is not the best way to begin non-symmetrical figures.

Here, for the record books, is another failure—a two-headed reindeer! (See Figure 2-14.)

2. After reviewing some of these pitfalls, a few practical suggestions would be in order. (See Figures 2-15A, 2-15B, 2-15C and 2-15D.) For this particular greeting card lesson, advise your class to make all drawings so that they touch the fold but do not touch the top, the outside, or the bottom edge of the folded paper.

2-14

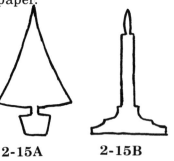

2-15A   **2-15B**   **2-15C**   **2-15D**

3. Both the cutout figure and the paper from which it is cut are used in the making of these greeting cards. The cutout becomes the inside decoration and the other piece becomes the cover. (See the illustration at the beginning of this lesson.)

If your kids are like mine, within minutes of the time that they "get the idea," your class will become as busy as a holiday assembly line!

concept
lesson 3   **The Sailboat Fold**

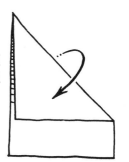

This fold has many uses. It is also the quickest way I know to make a perfect square. Later in this chapter I will show you how to use this same fold to make a cone.

you need:

• any rectangular sheet of paper

to present:

The Sailboat Fold. The Sailboat Fold is easier to do than it is to write about. The diagram above explains everything.

To Make a Square. Cut off the "sail" (S) from the "boat" (B) in Figure 2-16A. When part S is unfolded, it will be found to be a perfect square. (See Figures 2-16B and 2-16C.)

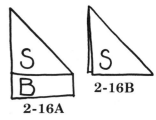

2-16A

2-16B

This square is also the beginning of a perfect nose—as you will see in the next lesson.

2-16C

referral
lesson 3   **Mask With a**
Sailboat-Nose

One of the problems with classroom how-to books is that the projects often call for a lot of precut paper pieces. As I have mentioned in the previous chapter, I don't believe in making the teacher's work any more difficult than necessary, so here is a way to save yourself one more trip to the papercutter—show your class how to use the Sailboat Fold to turn a rectangular piece of paper into a square.

you need:

- 6 x 4½" and 9 x 12" construction paper in assorted colors
- 6 x 4½" white mouth paper
- 3 x 9" colored hair paper
- scissors, paste or glue
- crayons (or other decorating materials)
- paper punch

to present:

1. Fold the 9 x 12" paper lengthwise. A little above halfway on the folded side, punch a hole through this double thickness of paper. Once the holes are punched, your class should have no difficulty poking their scissors through to enlarge the "eye-holes." (See Figure 2-17.)

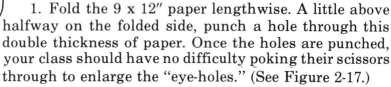

2-17

2. Make a square using the Sailboat Fold (see previous lesson) using one of the 6 x 4½" papers. Paste or glue this diagonally folded square to the head as shown in Figure 2-18. (Noses can be trimmed for a more realistic effect—but don't trim from the *folded* edge!)

3. Fold the white paper in half widthwise, unfold it and draw a mouth. Cut out this mouth and paste it into position while the mask is still in the folded position. (See Figure 2-19.)

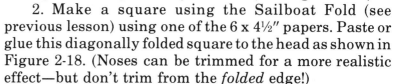

2-18

2-19

4. Divide one of the other 6 x 4½" papers in half to make ears. Fringe the 3 x 9" hair paper. (See Figure 2-20.) Paste ears and hair to head (as shown in the lead illustration) and encourage your kids to add any other details necessary to give added character to this mask.

Suggestions: Any mask idea can be given added life by doubling or even quadrupling the given measurements. The lead illustration suggests this possibility.

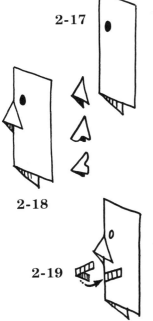

2-20

*concept
lesson 4*   **Circlecone**

Spherical forms are very difficult to make in paper. Wide-based Circlecones, however, make a pretty good substitute and can be used in dozens of different ways!

you need:

- a paper circle
- paste or glue

to present:

1. Draw a radius line as indicated, and cut on this line.

2. Paste A to overlap B and and your circlecone is complete. (See lead illustration.)

Further Suggestions: Since paper is not the world's strongest material, decorating an assembled Circlecone can be an object lesson in frustration, so either do your decorating *before* pasting the Circlecone, or use the corner of a table (see Figure 2-21) to support the sides while you work on them.

referral
lesson 4 A Circlecone Turtle

2-21

This turtle uses the Circlecone principle in two places, the head and the body. These turtles are fun to make, and with a little practice thay can even be made to "walk."

you need:

- 3½″ (watercup size) circle pattern
- white paper large enough to trace this pattern
- 6 x 9″ green paper
- paste, stapler, or glue
- crayons (or other decorating materials)

to present:

1. Have your kids trace the 3½″ circle pattern in the middle of the green paper. The next step is to have them draw in the numbers found on a clockface. (You'll find that it will go easier if you have them draw in the twelve, six, three, and nine first before attempting the intervening numbers.) Draw the turtle's head at twelve o'clock and the legs at two, four, eight, and ten o'clock as illustrated in Figure 2-22.

2-22

2-23

2. Draw another 3½" circle on the *white* paper. Paste this circle to the turtle's back and then draw a radius line from the center of this circle to the bottom of the turtle. Cut on this line (see heavy black line on Figure 2-23).

The turtle's back can be decorated now or after it is assembled. (See *Further Suggestions*, previous lesson.)

3. To give bounce to the turtle, fold on all dotted lines. (See Figure 2-24.) The parts fold *in* at the shell line and *out* on the other line.

2-24

4. Using the Circlecone principle of the previous lesson, assemble and paste the turtle. Again using the Circlecone principle, round the turtle's head. Cut a tail from the leftover scrap of green and paste it to the turtle's back end. Fold the tail in the same fashion as the legs were folded. Your turtle should now look like a close relative of the one pictured at the beginning of this lesson.

Operating Instructions: To put a little spring in the turtle's legs, playfully tap the turtle at the back of it's shell. Using this tapping motion, your turtle can be taught to "walk." It takes a little practice, but once you get it—it's fun to do!

concept
lesson 5   **Using Rulers and Straightedges**

I find that most kids cannot use a ruler properly. Either they cannot hold the ruler straight, take too few measurements, or ask disconcerting questions like, "Is it ten inches above the one in ten or is it one in front of it?" Or—they just simply goof. In any case, if you have ever experienced this kind of frustration in which two-thirds of the class are right with you and the other third is hopelessly lost, then you will appreciate this solution!

you need:

- ruler or tag strip
- pencil

to present:

To begin with, unless I want to end up teaching a combined art and math lesson, I avoid using the ruler for anything but drawing straight lines. This being the case, a traditional ruler is not even necessary. A tagboard or cardboard strip not only makes a satisfactory substitute, but is cheaper and in most ways just as effective.

If borders are needed, I simply tell the class to "draw a border as wide as the ruler (or straightedge) is wide." If it is necessary to have a border of a certain width, I pass out tagboard strips cut to size and use the same verbal directions.

*referral
lesson 5* **A Shadowbox
Picture Frame**

I use this basic box for more than framing pictures, and once you have seen its possibilities you will undoubtedly discover lots of other ways to put it to use.

you need:

- paper larger than the picture to be mounted
- pencil and ruler
- paste, glue, or stapler

to present:

1. Have your kids draw a border around the paper as wide as the ruler (or straightedge) is wide (see Figure 2-26), and press down hard with the pencil. (The hard pencil line is a form of *scoring*—see lesson 14, this chapter.)

2. Pressing down hard, draw diagonals to all four corners. (See Figure 2-26.) Fold up all sides and press in the corners as shown in Figure 2-27.

3. Using paste, glue, or a stapler, fasten all corners as

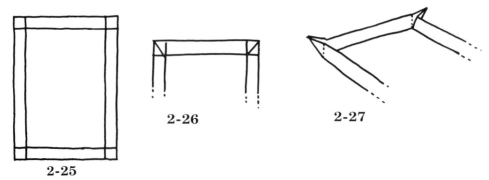

2-26   2-27

2-25

shown in lead illustration. With that, your shadowbox picture frame is complete!

Further Suggestions: When getting into areas that make for a mess (carving, glitter, etc.) these boxes make handy and disposable "work boxes."

concept
lesson 6 **Springs and How to Make Them**

Children love to make things that move, and if this movement adds an element of surprise—so much the better.

you need:

- paper strips in two contrasting colors
- paste

to present:

If you take your time, the two-piece spring can be successfully introduced even to first graders. But if you're in a hurry, the one-piece spring will make a satisfactory second-string substitute.

The One-Piece Spring

Have your class fold over the end of a long strip of paper. (See Figure 2-28A.) Next have them turn the paper over as shown in Figure 2-28B. Figures 2-28C and 2-28D

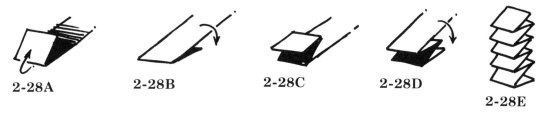

2-28A 2-28B 2-28C 2-28D

2-28E

repeat the two previous steps. By repeating this *up and over* two-step procedure, the strip will eventually become a folded "spring" as shown in Figure 2-28E.

The Two-Piece Spring

1. Have your kids paste their strips so that they form a right angle. (See Figure 2-29A.)
2. Using strips of contrasting colored paper is the secret to the successful presentation of this lesson, for all the kids have to learn is to overlap one color over another until there is no more paper left to fold! When that point is reached, paste the remaining flap. (See Figures 2-29B, 2-29C and 2-29D.)

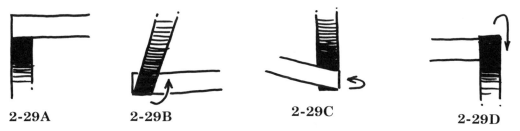

2-29A 2-29B 2-29C 2-29D

(The actual folding is easy—the diagrams make it look more difficult than it is.)

Teaching Tips for the Two-Piece Spring

1. Small children, particularly, must be reminded to fold "all the way." In other words, they must fold each strip snugly against the edge of the preceding strip.
2. Encourage your kids to keep their springs on their desks, for once their half-made springs "hit the air"— anything can happen!

WHE·E·E·E!

referral
lesson 6   **Spring Hoppers**

If you are looking for an easy lesson to use with the Two-Piece Springs, this is it. Small children love these perky creatures!

you need:

- 1 x 18″ strips of contrasting colors of construction paper (two each)
- paste or glue
- 6 x 4½″ drawing or construction paper
- crayons (or other decorating materials)

2-30A

to present:

1. On the 6 x 4½″ paper, have your kids draw and decorate some kind of a large friendly creature. When they are done have them cut it out. (See Figures 2-30A, 2-30B and 2-30C.)

2. The second and final part of this activity is simply to have them make a spring (see previous lesson) with the strips of construction paper and paste this spring to the underside of their creatures. In no time you'll have a room full of springing hoppers!

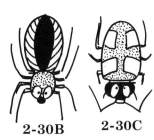

2-30B   2-30C

concept
lesson 7   **Three Ways of Curling Paper**

It is not enough to know *one* way to curl paper, because each of the *three* basic ways is in one way or another superior to the others!

you need:

- paper
- pencils
- scissors
- edge of a table (or any other large object with a fairly sharp edge)

to present:

Pencil Curls. The easiest way to curl long paper strips is by winding them around a pencil as in Figure 2-31. When the pencil is removed, the curls retain much of their shape. For curling narrow strips of paper, Pencil Curls work best.

Table-Edge Curls. For loose curls, this method works nicely. Simply pull the paper over the edge of a table with the palms of the hands as illustrated in Figure 2-32.

2-31

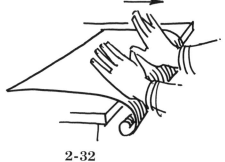

2-32

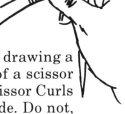

Scissor Curls. Scissor Curls are made by drawing a paper strip between the thumb and the side of a scissor blade. (See Figure 2-33.) The advantage of Scissor Curls lies in the speed with which they can be made. Do not, however, use Scissor Curls with paper that cannot take the brisk movement that this operation requires.

2-33

referral
lesson 7 **Curlies**

Pencil Curls (see previous lesson) are the secret in making these fun pictures!

you need:
- drawing paper
- narrow strips of paper
- paste, pencils, scissors
- crayons (or other decorating materials)

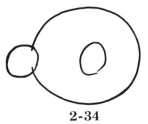

2-34

to present:

1. I doubt if your class needs any help drawing a head, but if they do, one large and two small circles make a good beginning for a fun-style cartoon head. (See Figure 2-34.)

2. The only advice that your kids will need for pasting the Pencil Curls is to apply them like shingles, that is, start at the bottom and work up. (See Figure 2-35.)

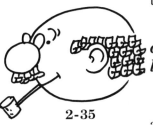

2-35

concept lesson 8   **Seeing Stars**

For young children, star making is not the easiest of activities. To give you a hand, here are three quick ways to stardom.

you need:

- paper
- pencil

to present:

Three Ways to Make a Star

2-36

1. *The Asterisk* (from the Greek *aster*, meaning star). An effective illusion of a small star can be made by using nothing more than an asterisk. (See Figure 2-36.)

2. *The Continuous-Line Star.* The traditional five-point star is usually drawn in one continuous line, but children facing this configuration for the first time can use all the help they can get! To make this star easier to remember, I have often used this mnemonic device. (See Figures 2-37A, 2-37B, 2-37C and 2-37D):

"First you make a mountain ...

"Go up to the left ...

"Across to the right ...

"And hurry back home!"

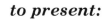

2-37A   2-37B

2-37C   2-37D

3. *The Five-Line Star.* Although this star is nothing more than a variation of the Continuous-Line Star, for some children it is easier to learn (see Figures 2-38A, 2-38B and 2-38C):

2-38A   2-38B

"First you make a mountain ...

"Draw a line that goes through the top of the mountain ...

"And add the two final crisscross lines!"

2-38C

referral
lesson 8   **Stars and Stripes Forever**

Children love flags, especially their own. This lesson is particularly appropriate for introducing the American flag to younger children. (In Chapter 5, you'll find an advanced flag-making project.)

you need:

- 3 x 4½″ blue construction paper (two each)
- 9 x 6″ white drawing or construction paper
- broken pieces of peeled red crayon
- scissors
- white chalk or white crayon
- 12 x 18″ drawing paper
- stapler, paste, or glue
- crayons (or other decorating materials)

to present:

1. Using the sides of broken pieces of peeled red crayons, have your class draw seven horizontal red stripes on both sides of the white paper as in Figure 2-39. (Since the American flag begins and ends with a red stripe, some of your kids may want to cut off any surplus white paper.)

2. Using white chalk or crayon, have your kids decorate each of the blue papers with stars. (See Figure 2-40.) Paste these blue fields to the same corresponding corner of each side of the striped paper.

3. Staple, paste, or glue the blue field edge of the flag

2-39

2-40

to the drawing paper and fold out the flag so that both sides can be seen.

4. Have your kids complete this activity by adding whatever else they feel is needed to complete the picture.

concept
lesson 9   **Full-Paper Star**

For many large-star projects, this Full-Paper Star works best for it produces a much more uniform star than the freehand star that I have described earlier in this chapter. I use this star for a lot of things!

you need:

 • pencil
 • paper

to present:

1. Have your class place a dot at the top of a vertical sheet of paper. Draw lines connecting this dot to the two bottom corners. (See Figure 2-41.)

2. The horizontal crossline should be drawn a little higher than halfway up the paper. This line should also touch both sides of the paper. (See Figure 2-42.)

3. And finally, complete the star by adding the two crisscrossing lines. (See Figure 2-43.)

   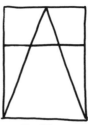      

2-41   2-42   2-43   2-44

Suggestions: Many children, especially the very young, cannot cut out this star (or any star) without removing at least one of its arms. The way around this stumbling block is to have your kids—step by directed step—lightly pencil scribble in the areas to be removed as in Figure 2-44. Kids enjoy this scribbling and, at the same time, it gives you a chance to catch a misplaced scribble— which is a lot easier to correct than an amputated star-arm!

referral
lesson 9 **The Star Witch**

The witch that stars in this activity is only one of a great many ways in which the versatile Full-Paper Star (see previous lesson) can be put to use!

you need:
- 9 x 12″ and a 3″ square of drawing or construction paper
- 6″ square and a 1 x 9″ strip of black construction paper
- paste, glue, or stapler
- crayons (or other decorating materials)

to present:
1. Have your class fold the 9 x 12″ paper in half lengthwise and very lightly pencil a Full-Paper Star (see previous lesson). Cut away shaded portions and paste the black strip to the bottom of the star as shown in Figure 2-45.
2. To finish the hat, draw a line a little below and parallel to the horizontal crossline of the star. Color the hat.

On the folded center of the pasted black strip, cut through the double thickness of paper.(See Figure 2-46.)

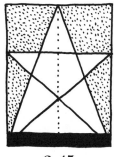

2-45

2-46

2-47

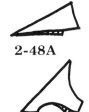

2-48A

2-48B

2-48C

3. Draw in the head, neck, etc., but when drawing in the face—leave room for a cut-paper nose! (See Figure 2-47.)

Have your kids fold the 3″ square in half, and draw and cut out some kind of a witch's nose. (Before turning them loose, however, it might be advisable to remind your kids of the basic rules of folded cut-paper cutting as outlined in lessons 3 & 4 of this chapter.) Some suggested nose shapes are presented in Figures 2-48A, 2-48B and 2-48C.

4. When the nose is complete, paste or glue it to overlap the folded face. Paste the completed witch to the 6″ black square as shown in the illustration at the beginning of this lesson.

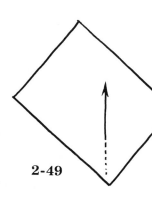

concept
lesson 10   **Making Paper Straws**

I can almost hear someone asking "Why?" Why would anyone want to make paper straws when you can buy straws for so little? The answer, of course, is that straw-making is fun and that *these* straws we are going to make differ in important ways from store-bought varieties!

you need:

- lightweight white paper (approx. 8½ x 11″)
- paste or glue
- scissors

to present:

1. Instruct your class to turn their papers on the diagonal so that the longest dimension (indicated in Figure 2-49 by a double-headed arrow) extends straight out from the straw-maker. With the paper placed in this direction, the apprentice straw-maker then tries to role up the straw in the direction indicated by the arrow.

2. Success can only be arrived at by practice, for rolling a thin paper straw is not easy. The secret is in getting off to a good start and in keeping enough tension

2-49

on the straw so that it stays together until the final touch of paste.

One way to roll a successful straw is to push with the fingers of one hand and use the thumb of the other hand as a "brake." (See lead illustration.)

3. Since the rolled straw ends up with a small free tab, the final pasting is easy. (See Figure 2-50.) If desired, the straw can be trimmed at each end.)

2-50

Uses for the Hand-Rolled Straw

This paper straw can be used in paper constructions in the same way that you would use any paper straw. Because of its heavy construction, it can also be used to make stumps or "shading sticks" which are useful for blending tones in drawings made with pencil, chalk, pastel, etc. For this purpose the stumps are best trimmed at each end and retrimmed as needed.

referral *lesson 10* **Blow Your Own Horn**

This is an old paper-folding trick—but it is the easiest way I know to put your straw-making abilities to work.

you need:

- 8½ x 11″ lightweight paper (duplicating paper will do)
- scissors
- paste or glue

to present:

1. Using the instructions from the previous lesson, roll a paper straw. Make two snips outward from point A in Figure 2-51A. The resulting triangular flap will become the vibrating end of the "horn." (See Figure 2-51B.)

2. To sound the horn, place the uncut end in your mouth, bend the triangular flap in slightly with your fingertip and suck in. A well-made horn will give off a

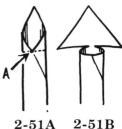

2-51A   2-51B

loud "mooing" sound. (Different lengths of paper will make for different sounds—experiment!)

The trick in mastering your horn is to suck in with just the right amount of pressure—too little and the flap does not vibrate, too much and the flap seals the tube completely.

concept
lesson 11   **Sailboat Cones**

In lesson 5 of this chapter, I showed you how to make the basic Sailboat Fold. This same fold is also the first step in the making of a couple of very useful cones!

you need:

- a rectangular piece of paper
- scissors
- pencil
- paste or glue

to present:

Start with the Sailboat Fold. (See Figures 2-52A and 2-52B.) Have your kids fold the "boat" upward as shown in Figure 2-52C and paste to the "sail." Turn the paper over to paste down remaining flap. (See Figure 2-52D.) With that—your basic Sailboat Cone is complete! (See Figure 2-52E.)

2-52A

2-52B

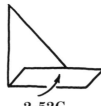

2-52C

2-52D

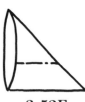

2-52E

Suggestions: If the cone is large enough, wear it as a hat. (See Figure 2-53A.)

Fill it with flowers and hang it on the wall. (See Figure 2-53B.)

 2-53A

 2-53B

The Perfect Sailboat Cone

If a perfectly symmetrical cone is needed you will have to trim off the shaded portion as shown in Figure 2-54. Rather than explain how to draw an arc, you might find it a lot easier to distribute a few prepared tagboard patterns (and save the arc concept for a math lesson).

2-54

referral
lesson 11 **The Sailboat Ghost**

It's too bad that Halloween comes but once a year because ghosts' activities are always popular with children.

you need:

- 12 x 18″ white drawing or construction paper
- assorted sizes of orange and black construction paper
- pencils, scissors, paste or glue
- crayons (or other decorating materials)
- scrap paper for stuffing

to present:

1. Make a perfect Sailboat Cone (see last paragraph, previous lesson) using the 12 x 18″ white paper. Save the paper that is trimmed away in the process.
2. Add eyes, mouth, and use the leftover scrap from step 1 to make the arms.
3. Make a ball of the scrap paper stuffing and push it

up inside the cone to give the ghost a full three-dimensional presence.

Suggestions: If you have orange and black paper on hand, your kids will not need much encouragement to "fix up" their ghosts with pumpkins, cats, trick-or-treat bags.

concept
lesson 12 **The Ins and Outs of
                      Cut Paper**

At its best there is nothing quite so decorative as cut paper. Those working in it for the first time, however, often encounter a variety of predictable problems. This lesson is designed to give you an insight into *why* these problems arise and to suggest ways in which you can help your class overcome these hurdles.

you need:

- colored paper
- scissors
- paste or glue

to present:

The great majority of problems arise from what artists call "positive and negative shapes." Although this fancy terminology is enough to frighten anyone, it is an easy concept to learn.

2-55

Take a look at Figure 2-55. The house is the positive shape; the space, the blank paper surrounding the house, is the negative shape. Making this house picture in cut-paper, most people would cut the house from a sheet of dark paper and paste it to the larger light-colored background sheet.

Now that you understand this concept, look at Figure 2-56A. The window is the positive shape, the space around it is the negative shape. Most people (including your kids) would approach the window in the same way as they solved the house problem, that is by cutting out the positive shape (the window) and pasting it to the larger background sheet. *And that's where the trouble begins!* (See Figure 2-56B.)

2-56A

Just because cutting out the window is the *natural* way of working does not mean that it's the best. The *easy* way is shown in Figure 2-57. The window panes are cut from white paper, pasted on a window-size piece of black paper, and the completed window is then mounted on the background paper.

2-56B

2-57

Another kind of related cut-paper problem is seen in Figure 2-58A. Although one *could* cut out the fence, the easy way is to cut out two long fence rails and the three

2-58A

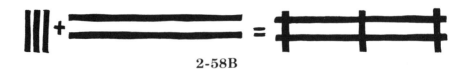

2-58B

fence posts separately and then assemble the fence as you're pasting it. (See Figure 2-58B.)

All of this sounds a lot more complicated than it is. That's because we are *talking* about a concept rather than *seeing* it. I can guarantee that you'll have no trouble presenting this material to your kids if you use actual sheets of cut paper in your demonstration. Once they understand the short-cuts, the rest is fun!

You might also mention to your class that since the paper that you are using is uniform in color, mistakes are easy to correct. Just cut off what you don't need and paste on what you want to change.

referral lesson 12   **The Basic Silhouette**

Generations of Americans have grown up associating the word *silhouette* with the mass produced and widely distributed silhouettes of Washington and Lincoln—yet the word silhouette comes from the last name of an 18th century French minister of finance. A silhouette is not necessarily a portrait, and there is no rule anywhere that states that it has to be done using black and white paper.

you need:

- two pieces of paper of contrasting colors (one or both of which could be black and/or white, but needn't be)
- scrap pieces in the same contrasting colors
- pencil
- scissors
- paste or glue

to present:

A silhouette lesson is fun, profitable, and highly decorative BUT it is not an easy lesson to present without a few sample silhouettes to use as examples. So before you try to introduce the silhouette concept, I would highly recommend that you take the time to locate some samples, or better yet, make a few yourself.

Guidelines for Making Silhouettes

1. Review the preceding lesson.
2. Discuss with your class the problem of the *groundline*. Silhouettes, as a rule, need a low groundline, as can be seen in Figures 2-59A and 2-59B:

with low groundline

with high groundline

2-59A

2-59B

3. Some views make better silhouettes than others—with people and animals, sideviews are generally better. (See Figures 2-60A and 2-60B.)

Some complicated things like houses are best translated into simple views. Compare, for example, the two houses below. (See Figures 2-61A, 2-61B, 2-61C and 2-61D.) Silhouette 2-61B ends up looking like a house; 2-61D looks more like a barn!

2-60A   2-60B

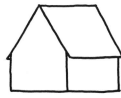

2-61A   2-61B   2-61C   2-61D

2-62A

2-62B

4. Also point out to your class that silhouettes can be just as easily done with white on black as with black on white. (See Figures 2-62A and 2-62B.)

5. When you have finished paving the way, turn your class loose on a silhouette of their own invention. The results will delight you!

concept
lesson 13   **Color Magic**

To those who are sensitive to color, nothing is more jarring than its misuse. Some people have a natural understanding of what makes color harmony but many of the rest of us have profited from an exposure to a little theory. Some of the most valuable lessons are outlined in the paragraphs below.

you need:

- crayons (or other decorating materials)

to present:

Despite their love for color, many kids massacre it. They like the physical act of applying color—full strength—and they take great interest in reacquainting themselves with each color in turn, but the end results are often disastrous. This is particularly true of more ambitious paintings in the higher grades than the paintings done by younger children (a quickly done, freely sketched picture can generally take care of itself). Recognizing their inability to handle color, many older children show their sensitivity to it by avoiding it entirely. At this point, color theory can save the day!

Primary Colors. The study of color begins with what artists call the *primary* colors: red, yellow, and blue. These colors can be mixed to make the *secondary* colors: orange, green, and violet.

red + yellow = orange
yellow + blue = green
blue + red = violet

The Color Wheel. The color wheel is a way in which all of this can be explained in visual terms. The secondary colors are sandwiched between the larger parent or primary colors.

Colors directly opposite each other on this color wheel (such as orange and blue) produce browns. Browns can also be made by mixing all colors together. (See Figure 2-63.)

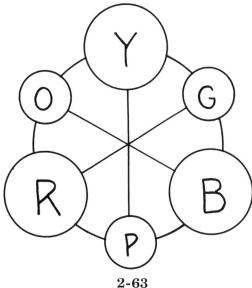

2-63

Color Schemes. A color scheme is a recipe for color success. Here are three good ones:

1. A *monochromatic* color scheme is a color scheme that uses shades of the same color. For example, dark blue slacks and light blue blouse, or a picture that is done all in shades of blue.

2. An *analogous* color scheme is a color scheme that uses colors that neighbor each other on the color wheel, such as yellow, green, and blue, or red, orange, and yellow.

3. A *pastel* color scheme uses colors that are considerably less than full strength and are therefore much softer and more delicate in feeling than colors used at their full intensity.

When using poster paint, acrylics, etc., this "change-it-with-white" color scheme is a good rule of thumb that goes a long way towards getting rid of the usual park-bench greens, fire-engine reds, and soda-pop purples!

referral
lesson 13 **Seven-Line Cubism**

If you are looking for a lesson that is easy to present and whose end results are really impressive, this is the lesson for you! Because of its sure-fire decorative qualities, it may well become one of your favorites.

you need:

- paper and pencils
- rulers or straightedges
- 9 x 12″ drawing paper
- crayons (or other decorating materials)

2-64

2-65

to present:

1. Have your class lightly pencil a picture idea on their drawing paper. Suggest that they make their drawings large and without a great deal of detail as in Figure 2-64.

2. Using rulers or straightedges have your kids draw three straight nonparallel overlay lines in one direction and four in the other. (See Figure 2-65.)

3. Now the tricky part begins! Review a little bit of color theory, especially the part about *analogous* color (see previous lesson). Then have your kids choose *three* analogous colors plus black. Explain that the rules of this

activity are that these are the only colors that they are allowed to use.

4. The problem: to color their pictures with only these colors used straight or mixed, applied lightly or darkly. However—*they have to change color each time they cross a line, any line!* Make sure that your kids understand that you mean *any* line and not just the seven overlay lines.

When done with love and care, this activity produces a picture that shimmers with dozens of harmoniously chosen compartments of color, and as such it makes a perfect introduction to much of Twentieth century modern art.

concept
lesson 14   **Paper Scoring**

Paper folds only in straight lines: true or false? If you answered *true* to the above question then it's time that you learned about paper scoring!

you need:

- paper
- pencils
- scissors, or anything else with a sharp (but not too sharp) point

to present:

To *score* is to groove the paper as a preparatory step to ensure accurate folding. For example, it's easier to fold a piece of paper along a predetermined line if that line is drawn with a sharp pencil applied with more than usual pressure. This pressure makes a groove that weakens the paper wherever the line is drawn, thereby preparing the way for the folding operation.

Since it is not the pencil lead but the pressured point that grooves the paper, you can use a nail, a nailfile, or anything else that has a reasonably sharp point.

For folding cardboard or heavyweight papers, scoring is invaluable. However, the full potential of scoring is not seen until you begin to experiment with the scoring of *curved* lines. Here beautiful things can be done!

Try the experiments pictured below: score on the dotted lines and carefully fold (one segment at a time) on the scored lines. (See Figures 2-66A, 2-66B and 2-6-6C.)

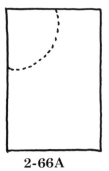 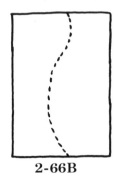 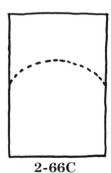

2-66A   2-66B   2-66C

The illustrations at the beginning of this lesson cannot begin to do justice to these scored figures. Carefully done, scoring is a beautiful activity.

Suggestions: Try having your class make their own scored inventions and hang them from the ceiling!

referral
lesson 14   **Autumn Leaves**

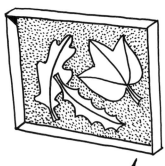

Here is ample opportunity for your class to put their scoring skills to work, and at the same time turn your room into a blaze of autumn!

you need:

- 9 x 12″ brown construction paper
- 6 x 4½″ and 12 x 15″ construction paper in assorted autumn colors
- rulers or tagboard straightedges (preferably over 15″ in length)
- stapler, paste or glue

to present:

1. Give each child a variety of assorted 6 x 4½″
2-67A autumn colors and have them draw one leaf on each

sheet. Some suggested leaf shapes might include Figures 2-67A, 2-67B and 2-67C.

Score (see previous lesson) the gracefully curved centerlines of each leaf. (On some leaves, such as the maples, more than one line can be scored.) Cut out the leaves and fold on the scored lines.

2. Using a ruler or straightedge, draw a border "as wide as the ruler is wide" around the edge of the 12 x 15″ paper, and from this prepare a Shadowbox (see referral lesson 5, this chapter). Paste the 9 x 12″ brown paper inside the completed box and paste in the scored leaves to make a decorative autumn design.

2-67B

2-67C

concept
lesson 15   **End-Cones**

Of all the "tricks" in this chapter, I probably use the End-Cones the least—but don't prejudge them too quickly because when you need an End-Cone, there is nothing else that can do the job!

you need:

- paper
- paste
- glue or stapler

to present:

Single End-Cones. Place a dot one-half way between the corners of one of the short sides. (See Figure 2-68A.) Overlap the corners nearest the dot and paste. (See Figure 2-68B.) That's it!

Double End-Cones. The same instructions can be used at both ends to produce the Double End-Cone shown in Figure 2-69A. (The inverted Double End-Cone, see Figure 2-69B, is the basic shape upon which the next lesson is based.)

2-68A

2-68B

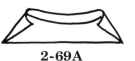

2-69A

2-69B

2-70

Open End-Cone. Occasionally an activity calls for a loosely made or Open End-Cone. Such a cone is pictured in Figure 2-70.

referral
lesson 15 **End-Cone Fish
and Fowl**

This activity uses the Double End-Cone (see previous page) to good advantage. These creatures are easy to make, fun to look at, and if you enlarge the basic paper size to approximately 12 x 15″, your class can wear them as hats!

you need:

- 9 x 12″ construction paper in one color and a number of 6 x 4½″ pieces in a contrasting color
- scissors, and paste, glue, or stapler
- crayons (or other decorating materials)
- and for the bird only, a 2 x 4″ piece of yellow paper

to present:

The Fish

1. The fish begins with a 9 x 12″ Double End-Cone. The large "smile" that is the tail fin of the fish is cut from one of the 6 x 4½″ pieces. It is attached by means of a vertical slot cut into the tip of one of the End-Cones. (See Figure 2-71.)

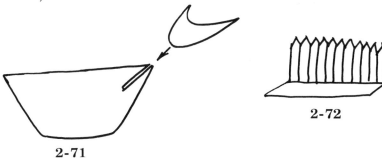

2-71

2-72

2. The back, or dorsal, fin is made by folding a piece of paper to form an L or "pasting foot" as in Figure 2-72. This "foot" is either pasted onto the back of the fish or, better still, inserted into the fish through a slot cut in the back and pasted inside the fish. The bottom, or anal, fin can be handled in the same way.

3. When the remaining fins, the triangular pelvic and pectoral fins, are cut out and pasted into position, your fish is done!

The Bird

1. The bird too is constructed from a Double End-Cone but unlike the fish the End-Cone paper needs some prior preparation. Have your kids draw a semicircle to one of the short ends of your End-Cone paper as shown in Figure 2-73.

2. Then—turn this sheet of paper into a Double End-Cone. Add an eye on each side of the head and a line to divide the beak. (See Figure 2-74.)

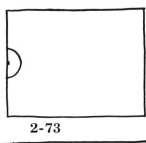

2-73

2-74

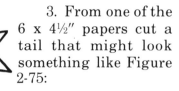

2-75

3. From one of the 6 x 4½″ papers cut a tail that might look something like Figure 2-75:

4. From two more 6 x 4½″ papers cut two wings which could look like Figure 2-76:

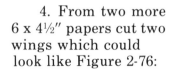

2-76

5. The bird's back end is slotted slantwise to accommodate the tail, and the wings are either pasted on flat or pasted so that they extend outward. (See Figure 2-77.) That's it!

2-77

concept lesson 16   **Basic Weaving**

The fascinating thing about weaving lies in the knowledge that the color and pattern possibilities are infinite! Here is as basic an approach as you'll ever find.

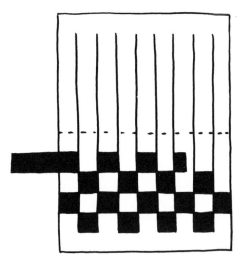

you need:

- 9 x 12″ construction paper in two contrasting colors
- pencil and ruler or straightedge (preferably about 1″ in width)
- scissors, and paste or glue

to present:

The Warp. In weaving, the long threads (or strips) are called the *warp*. Here is how the warp is prepared for this lesson.

1. Using one of the sheets of 9 x 12″ paper, have your kids draw a straight line "as wide as the ruler (or straightedge) is wide" along one of the short edges. (See Figure 2-78A.) Once drawn, have the paper folded in half widthwise so that the pencil line is on the outside. (See Figure 2-78B.) Then draw a series of lines perpendicular to the first line to make strips which are again "as wide as the ruler is wide." (See Figure 2-78C.) Cut on these perpendicular lines. When opened, the resulting long strips of paper will become the warp. (See Figure 2-78D.)

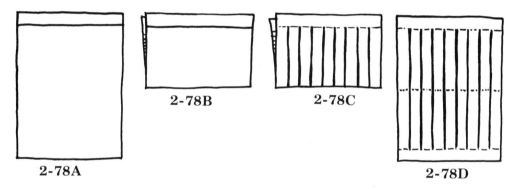

2-78B   2-78C

2-78A   2-78D

The Weft. In weaving, the short threads (or strips) are called the *weft*. To make the weft for this lesson, simply draw widthwise lines, on the other sheet of 9 x 12″ paper, as wide as the ruler is wide and cut on these lines.

Learning to Weave: The weaving process itself is so well-known that I don't think I have to describe it to my readers. It is basically an in and out process that reverses itself every other row. (With kids, you'll find yourself using expressions like "in and out the window.") But although weaving may seem simple to you, to some children this is a highly complex process. In my experience, however, once the child can get through the first couple of rows, the battle is won.

For very small children, see *World's Easiest Weaving* p.100.

As paradoxical as it may sound, it is sometimes easier to teach this lesson with *two* weft colors, for once the first two rows of weft go on, the child can then concentrate on seeing that all blue rows imitate the first blue strip and all red rows imitate the second red strip.

Final Operations:

"The Squeeze." Few things can be as frustrating to a young child as weaving that begins to fall apart. To combat this possibility I use my fingernails on their weaving to pull the weft together. I call it *squeezing*, which is a good child-oriented word, for it loans itself to all kinds of humorous situations. ("Mr. Baer, I'm ready to be squeezed!)

"The Shoelace." Once the weaving is complete and squeezed to the point that it cannot take another standard strip, suggest trimming one of the remaining weft strips to make a "shoelace." When the shoelace has been threaded through the last bit of warp, have your kids paste down all of the loose weft ends and the weaving is complete.

referral
lesson 16 **Skip-Weaving**

This advanced weaving is fun to do and a lot easier than it looks!

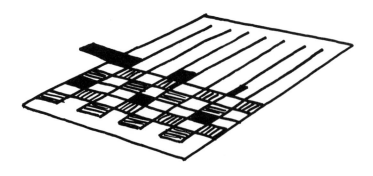

you need:

- four different colors or shades of construction paper in the following sizes:
    - one 12 x 18"
    - three 6 x 12"
- pencil and ruler (or straightedge)
- scissors, and paste or glue

to present:

1. Prepare a 12 x 18" warp and 12" weft strips as explained in the previous lesson.

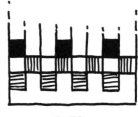

2-79

2. Now comes the fun. The instructions are as follows: each of the three *weft* colors are woven in sequence but each follows a different weaving pattern. For example, all yellow strips might go "in and out," all green strips might go "out and in," and all blue strips might go "in one and out *two*." (See Figure 2-79.)

When this weaving is complete and the loose edges are pasted down, you'll have as nice an example of paper weaving as you will ever see!

Comments: Although this activity opens up all kinds of vistas, it is possible for a child to follow the instructions to the letter and fail. What can happen is this: unless one checks part way through to see that each warp strip has been engaged on *both* sides by the weft, the child could complete the weaving only to discover long unengaged warp strips on the reverse side of the woven mat.

Fortunately, there is a way to guarantee perfect results—make sure that two of the three weft strips are reverses of each other. For example, one strip should be an "in and out" pattern while the other follows the "out and in" pattern.

Although all of this sounds complicated, the results are well worth the trouble!

3

Starting with the Very Young

Although this chapter is primarily designed for children who are just learning how to control crayons, manipulate scissors, and apply paste, you'll soon find that there is an abundance of valuable material here for everyone! Since a good lesson is not easily inhibited by the artificial barriers of age and grade level, I have loaded this section with suggestions and recommendations for adapting these ideas to other levels of instruction. So whether you teach the very young or those of advanced skills and abilities, here are over two dozen good lessons just waiting for *your* kids to bring them to life!

concept
lesson 1   # The Gentle Art
                 # of Pasting

If you are working with a new group, the wisest course of action is to assume that pasting instructions are necessary—to assume otherwise is to invite disaster! Just because your group *looks* reasonably mature does not mean that they have any degree of savvy when it comes to a common sense use of paste. I have seen fourth graders who knew less about pasting than many preschoolers. The difference? A little instruction!

you need:

- one large sheet of paper, two smaller pieces
- paste

to present:

When instructing the very young, I begin by assuming nothing. In this case, many may be seeing paste for the first time in their young lives and others may not be far removed from their first experience.

First Pasting Lesson

1. Explain to your class that you are about to paste a small piece of paper to a larger sheet. Now comes the question: should you put the paste on the big piece of paper or on the smaller one? After recognizing a few opinions, put the matter to a vote.

2. Once the vote is in, explain with great tact that those who voted for putting the paste on the smaller piece were right and those who voted for putting the paste on the larger paper were wrong. (In five-year old minds, for example, the announcement that one group is right does not necessarily mean that the others were wrong unless you make a point of saying so!) Then proceed to demonstrate this point by using both methods to paste down the two small pieces of paper. One, of course, goes on neatly and adroitly while the other (and I make sure of this) is a complete and obvious mess. With that—a little bit of cheating and a great deal of showmanship—your point is made!

Second Pasting Lesson

Without some kind of firm guidelines, pasting can lead to a room full of sticky hands, tacky furniture, and paste-smeared clothes. There *is* an alternative:

1. When you finish with the First Pasting Lesson, you are left with a dab of paste on the end of your index finger. NOW is the time to begin Speech Number Two. When I do it, it goes something like this: "When pasting, some people get paste all over their hands, and then do you know what they do? They wipe their hands all over their clothes! When they get home, wow, do they get in trouble! But not *me!* I don't want to get in trouble with my mother!* So let me show you how *I* do it!"

3-1

Once you have set the scene, explain how you use only one finger for pasting—the index finger. Show how most of the paste remaining on the end of this finger can be wiped off onto the paste pad (or into the paste jar). Explain that although your finger now *looks* nearly paste free, it is still a little sticky. The solution? Simply wipe this sticky finger on the *back* of the other hand. (See Figure 3-1.) The back of the hand is probably the safest place in the room for paste. Here it dries quickly and cannot get on your clothes, your hair or your paper! Try to illustrate this point with as much memorable dramatics as you can muster, for if your kids can remember this procedure for handling paste, most of your pasting troubles are over!

The alternatives to having your kids use the back of their hands for paste are hardly worth considering: paste brings out the worst in Kleenex-style paper tissues; having your kids run back and forth to the sink is to encourage the constant distraction of unnecessary movement; and to do nothing is to become the eternal enemy of all washday mothers. So for those of you who have never learned to use the back of the hand for wiping off the last vestiges of paste—this tip alone should be worth the price of this book!

---

*With most small children a line like this doesn't even make a ripple. They live with their mothers so why shouldn't a married man with a wife and four kids live with his mother? Rather than sounding like a weak joke, the whole concept makes for immediate identification—it makes me one of the gang!

lesson 2   **A Simple Starter**

Here is one of the easiest, as well as one of the best, introductory lessons I know. It allows each child to work at his own pace and it gives the teacher an ample opportunity to observe the different personalities at work. And as a measure of creativity, it ranks somewhere near the top!

you need:

- 12 x 18″ drawing paper
- a variety of precut, odd-shaped pieces of colored paper
- paste or glue
- crayons (or other decorating materials)

to present:

For the Very Young

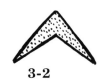

3-2

Hold up an odd-shaped piece of colored paper. Keep turning this paper in your hand so your class can look at the paper from different viewpoints. The big question comes when you ask: "What does it look like?"

For example, let us say that Figure 3-2 is the shape in question:

Some will say that it looks like a pair of pants, others will see a bird, or a rooftop, etc. When the volunteered ideas begin to wear thin, paste this shape on *your* paper, and once pasted take a crayon and make something out of it. For example, Figure 3-3 could be your answer.

3-3

Repeat the process once again until everyone understands how the "game" is played, then invite each child to select an odd-shaped piece from your precut assortment and begin. Each time they complete a shape invite them back for another which they can then paste to the same sheet. (For those who show a lack of imaginative skills, I cheat a bit by occasionally handing out easy shapes, shapes that are purposely cut out with simple, familiar forms in mind.) A finished paper might look something like Figure 3-4.

3-4

For the More Experienced

This lesson needs little or no adaptation for older children. The only major difference in classroom re-actions will be for the older child to want to spend a relatively longer time turning the starter into a picture complete with background. To anticipate the needs of your older class, encourage them in this direction.

lesson 3   **Things That Fly**

Adults are inclined to think of art in terms of galleries and museums, but young children are not so stuffy. They draw no hard line between art and life. The things they make are not meant primarily to be viewed—they are meant to be given, to be played with, or to be shown to others. This lesson is meant to be played with, and to watch young children as they learn to "fly" these graceful creatures is an object lesson in living!

Butterflies for the Very Young

you need:

- 12″ square of drawing or construction paper and a 3 x 6″ piece in a contrasting color
- 1 x 6″ strip of black paper
- stapler and a small amount of paste
- crayons (or other decorating materials)

to present:

1. Instruct your class in the art of making a diagonal fold. Have them fold the 12″ square diagonally and cut this fold to make two triangles.

2. Have the 3 x 6″ paper folded lengthwise and staple the triangular "wings" to the body as shown in Figure 3-5.

3. While you are busy stapling, have your class cut two thin strips for antennae. After the body and the wings have been assembled, the antennae can then be pasted in the "head." Eyes and other details or decorative touches can be added at any time. (See illustration at the beginning of this lesson.)

3-5

Flying Instructions: The first advice is a *don't—* don't fold the wings. Hold the body in your hand and *spread* the wings out gently into a flying position. Now very slowly move your hand up and down, and this paper creature will re-create in a wonderful fashion the graceful movements of a real butterfly.

Birds—for the slightly more experienced

you need:

- 9″ square of construction paper
- 3 x 9″ construction paper (same color as the 9″ square)
- 6 x 12″ construction paper in a contrasting color
- small piece of yellow paper
- stapler, and paste or glue
- crayons (or other decorating materials)

to present:

1. The 9″ square is to be folded diagonally and cut on the fold. The resulting triangles will become wings.

2. The 6 x 12″ paper is to be folded lengthwise to form the body, the 3 x 9″ widthwise to make the tail. Fold the tail in half and then assemble and staple into the basic bird shown in Figure 3-6.

3. Trim the body until it becomes more bird-like. Fold down the tail, add a beak from yellow paper, add an eye on each side, and legs if desired, etc.

4. Using the *Flying Instructions* from the previous lesson, your birds are ready to take to the air!

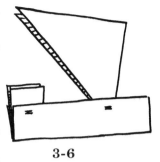

3-6

lesson 4   The Picnic Lunch

Very few things in life approach perfection—but The Picnic Lunch is as close to the perfect lesson as you will ever find! Teachers of older children, however, will have to look elsewhere for the perfect lesson—this picnic lunch is only for the very young.

you need:

• construction or drawing paper in the following colors and sizes:

    4½ x 6″ manila hot dog bun paper
    9 x 3″ brown hot dog paper
    4½ x 6″ brown hamburger paper
    9 x 6″ manila hamburger roll paper
    3″ squares white bread paper (two each)
    4½ x 12″ white milk paper
    4½ x 6″ red tomato paper
    4½ x 6″ yellow-green lettuce paper
    small pieces of green pickle paper

• paper lunch bag

• 3½″ (watercup size) circle pattern

• pencil, stapler, scissors, and crayons (or other decorating materials)

to present:

The order of presentation here is unimportant, for whatever the order the kids will "eat it up."

3-7

The Hot Dog. The frankfurter is drawn on the brown paper and cut out. The manila paper is folded in half lengthwise to make the bun. Once the sandwich has been assembled it can be decorated with mustard, ketchup, or relish (with a yellow, red, or green crayon.)

The Hamburger. The hamburgers are made by tracing the circle pattern on the brown paper and having your kids cut them out. The hamburger roll is a little more complicated; the roll paper is folded in half widthwise and the circle pattern is drawn as shown in Figure 3-7, with the pattern extending beyond the center fold of the paper. Have your kids cut out the roll, put in the hamburger and then add the following extra ingredients as desired:

Tomato. For those who like tomato on their hamburger, have them cut out a circle from the red paper.

Lettuce. For those who like lettuce, have them tear out a piece of lettuce from the yellow-green paper.

Pickle. Pickle lovers are encouraged to cut out as many pickles as they please.

Peanut Butter Sandwiches. Have your kids spread peanut butter (brown crayon) on one piece of bread and their favorite jelly-color on the other.

Glass of Milk. Roll the milk paper into glass-size cylinders and staple. Be sure to remind your kids not to spill their milk! They love this make-believe scolding.

And Then—put everything in their lunch bags so they can take their picnic home!

lesson 5　**A Call to Columbus**

For young children even a simplified Columbus boat can become a major boat-building experience. Here is one of the best paste and paper caravels.

you need:

* construction paper in the following colors and sizes:

For more advanced Columbus lessons see *The Happy Holidays*, pp. 144-145.

12 x 18" light blue background
4 x 9" brown boat paper
4½ x 6" yellow mainsail
1½ x 9" red
4½ x 6" white cloud paper

- scissors, and paste or glue

- crayons (or other decorating materials)

to present:

1. Begin by having your class draw and cut out of the boat paper the shape shown in Figure 3-8. Since the finished boat bears a superficial resemblance to a telephone, I enjoy letting this phone "ring," and while the kids are cutting out their boats I carry on an imaginary conversation with Christopher discussing the coming holiday.

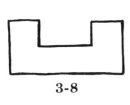

3-8

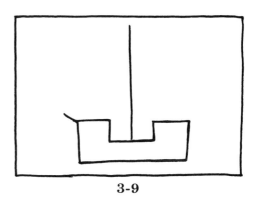

3-9

2. The bow of the boat can be pointed or left as is, but either way it is pasted near the bottom of the paper. The mast and the bowsprit are then drawn on with crayons. (See Figure 3-9.) After the mast is drawn, add the mainsail. The red cross is made by folding the red paper in half widthwise, cutting it, and then pasting the overlapping pieces to the sail. The cloud (or clouds) can be torn from the white paper, and the V-birds and water are added with crayon. The rudder can be made from the rectangle saved from the brown boat paper.

Have your class add as many other details as they can think of: railings, portholes, anchor, sailors, etc.

lesson 6   **A Magic Trace of Autumn**

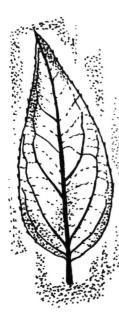

Autumn makes a wonderful opportunity to introduce crayon rubbing in its simplist form. The strength of this particular lesson is in the magic of its presentation. With just a little bit of showmanship, a sheet of paper, a peeled crayon, and a leaf—a great deal of learning can take place!

To be a magician to the very young is easy if you remember that a great deal of what you take for granted is often a real mystery to even the brightest child.

you need:

- 12 x 18″ drawing paper
- crayons with their wrappers removed
- autumn leaves

to present:

Begin by taking your class outside to collect leaves—the greater the variety the better. When your class has returned from their nature walk, have them gather around while you perform a miracle.

1. Casually hold up a folded sheet of paper and a peeled crayon and announce that you are the world's fastest artist. With that, lay down your paper and demonstrate how you can instantaneously draw a beautiful leaf with nothing but the side of your crayon and a few quick rubbing motions.

Naturally, since this is to be their first introduction to crayon rubbings, all will be properly impressed with your "artistic" talents. After everyone has had ample time to admire your work, then—show them the trick. *Inside* the folded sheet of paper is a hidden leaf! Demonstrate it again, only this time with everyone's full knowledge of the hidden leaf. Instantly everyone will want to fold their papers to become magic leaf artists!

2. After your kids have used up one side of their folded papers, have them turn their papers over to use the other side. Since many of your kids would not have thought of this themselves, your instructions will be gratefully received. When they have finished the second

side and are asking for more paper, your second miracle takes place.

Announce your next "trick" with all of the aplomb with which you announced your first. You explain to your class that you can turn an old sheet of paper into a new sheet. As you say this, pick up one of the "finished" sheets, show that it is used on both sides, turn your back for an instant to your audience and *presto!*—you turn holding up a "new" sheet of clean, folded paper!

A good percentage of your kids will be absolutely dumbfounded by your act of turning their used sheet inside-out, and those few who see through your trick will be delighted with your cleverness. Your two "tricks" are sure to be counted among the successes of the day!

For the More Experienced. All kinds of repeat patterns are possible, especially when one begins to alternate colors and leaf patterns. For advanced crayon rubbings see *Pictures for Rubbing,* p. 134.

lesson 7   **Triangle Fun**

From an adult point of view this particular activity may not seem like much of a problem—but from a little kid's point of view, there is a lot to be learned from this investigation of the triangle!

you need:

- 12 x 18" dark construction paper
- 2" squares of brightly colored construction paper
- scissors, and paste or glue
- and possibly a pencil

to present:

This activity is easy to present, for all that you are asking the kids to do is cut on the diagonal to turn squares into triangles. These triangles are then pasted on a larger sheet of paper.

Naturally, some small children will have trouble with the whole concept of cutting on a diagonal. Have these children draw the diagonal first with a pencil and then cut on the pencil line.

But most of your kids will get the idea right away and will get right down to the fascinating business of exploring the relationships formed by pasting one triangle against another.

Triangle Fun for the More Experienced. While younger children will be delighted just with the abstract relationships of pasted triangles, older children can be encouraged to arrange their triangles to create pictures. The potential of these triangle pictures is nearly unlimited when the larger triangles are snipped into smaller triangles. (See Figure 3-10.)

3-10

lesson 8 **The Pumpkin Family**

Pumpkins are always popular. Here is a whole family of them!

you need:

- construction paper in the following colors and sizes:*
    - black—12 x 18″ and 6 x 4½″
    - orange—6 x 9″, 4½ x 6″, 4½ x 3″
    - brown—scrap pieces
- paste or glue
- pencils, scissors, and perhaps a black crayon

to present:

1. Have your class draw and cut out a large pumpkin shape using the largest piece of orange paper. The eyes, nose, and mouth are drawn on the smaller sheet of black paper, cut out, and pasted on the pumpkin head. By adding a piece of scrap brown for a stem, the completed pumpkin is ready to be pasted to the horizontal sheet of black paper. This is the "father" pumpkin.

2. Repeat the same process with the 4½ x 6″ sheet of orange paper to make the "mother" pumpkin, which is also added to the black paper.

3. The Pumpkin Family is complete when the kids turn the smallest piece of orange paper into the "baby" pumpkin.

For the More Experienced. For the very young this lesson needs no further embellishments, but for slightly older children you might take the time to show your kids the "easy" way to add teeth, pupils to the eyes, etc. (See *The Ins and Outs of Cut Paper, p. 54.)*

Older children will be interested in discovering how just a few lines can transform a childlike drawing into a realistic pumpkin of considerable charm. The longitudinal crayon lines that transform a flat pumpkin into a plumper one (see Figure 3-11) are self-explanatory, easy to learn, and add a whole new dimension to the making of classroom pumpkins.

3-11

---

*All are approximate sizes. As explained in Chapter 1, I believe in cutting paper so that it leaves usable remainders. All of the paper sizes here (and almost everywhere else in this book) follow this rule.

lesson 9   **Triangle-Eye Mask**

Masks are popular at any age. Here is one that is neither too demanding nor too easy. For young children—it's "just right."

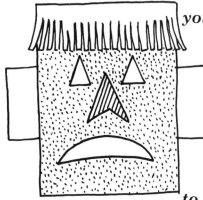

you need:

- construction paper in the following colors and sizes:
    - 9 x 12″ asssorted light colors
    - 6 x 4½″ white mouth
    - 3 x 4½″ red nose
    - 6 x 4½″ assorted "ear" paper (optional)
    - 3 x 9″ assorted dark hair paper
- paste or glue, pencils, scissors, and crayons (or other decorating materials)

to present:

Since the eyes have to be precut, this mask takes a little advanced preparation on *your* part. Using a sharp instrument like a single-edged razor blade, cut out triangular-shaped eyes in the 9 x 12″ paper. (You can probably cut as many as five or six sheets at a time.) The eyehole placement is not crucial although I would recommend that the eyes be placed a little above center.

The *white paper*—have the kids draw, cut out, and paste on a mouth. Teeth of course, are optional.

The *red paper*—the nose can be any fanciful shape.

The *hair paper*—can be fringed before pasting to the top.

The *ear paper*—ears are optional, for they are not missed on a mask. However, if time permits, they are fun to do. Divide the ear paper in half and add when ready.

Additional suggestions might include adding details such as eyebrows and rounding the corners of the mask to change the appearance.

For the More Experienced. For the slightly more experienced class I often use a paper punch to make a starting hole for the kids to enlarge into eye holes. (See *Sailboat-Nose Mask*, p. 37.)

Teachers of older children will find an assortment of more advanced masks elsewhere in this book.

lesson 10   **Pilgrim Mother**

This activity combines a number of simple skills into an engaging Pilgrim that can easily serve as a stand-up holiday centerpiece.

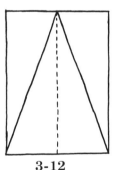

you need:

- 6 x 4½" and 1½ x 6" pieces of the same dark-colored construction paper
- 3" squares of assorted skin-toned construction paper (two each)
- 2" square and ¾ x 6" strip of white paper
- paste or glue
- crayons (or other decorating materials)

to present:

1. Have your class draw a large circle on one of the pieces of skin-toned paper. After adding features and long hair, have your kids cut out this head.

2. The 6 x 4½" dress paper is to be folded lengthwise and lines are then drawn from the top end of this fold to the two lower corners. (See Figure 3-12.) Cut on these lines. The largest triangle will become the body.

3. Have your kids paste the head to the body and add arms by pasting the 1½ x 6" strip across the back. The 2" square becomes the apron. Pieces are snipped off the ¾ x 6" strip to make collar and cuffs. For hands, oval shapes can be cut out of the second piece of skin-toned paper.

4. When the paste has had half a chance to dry, the Pilgrim Mothers can be folded down the middle and made to stand.

3-12

For the More Experienced. This lesson crosses grade lines easily. Older children can either elaborate on the figure or even incorporate it into a diorama (see *Dioramas*—Thanksgiving style, p. 156).

lesson 11   **Pilgrim Father**

What better to accompany a Pilgrim Mother than a Pilgrim Father? Although this lesson is a little more complicated than the previous one, if you take it one step at a time it will be as easy as pie!

you need:

- 6 x 2¼″ and 1 x 6″ strip of the same pilgrim clothes construction paper
- 3″ squares of skin-toned construction paper (two each)
- ¾ x 6″ strip of white paper
- small pieces of black shoe paper
- scissors, and paste or glue
- crayons (or other decorating materials)

to present:

1. Have your kids fold the 6 x 2¼″ pilgrim paper widthwise, unfold it, and fold it again lengthwise. Cut on the heavy lines. (See Figure 3-13.) The basic body is now complete.

2. One of the 3″ squares is for the drawing of the head. The cut-out head and the 1 x 6″ arm paper is then pasted to the body.

3. Discuss the location for the belt line and draw same.

4. Color the pilgrim's stockings and add black paper shoes.

3-13

5. Cut off pieces from the white paper to make cuffs, collar, and assorted buckles.

6. From the second piece of skin-toned paper cut out hands and paste to the end of the arms.

For the Slightly More Experienced. Older children will enjoy folding the figure at the knees, hips, and elbows and folding the feet outward to allow this little man to assume a number of realistic positions. Once limbered by these folds, try having this Pilgrim perform a funny dance step. Your class will love it!

Here are two other ideas that will be of interest to your class:

Buckles. An improved buckle can be made by simply coloring in the center of the white buckle paper with a black crayon as in Figure 3-14, or by using the folded paper method.

3-14

Pilgrim Hats. Older children will simply draw their hats and cut them out. Younger children will need help. Here is a way to construct a very simple hat—just have the kids paste a strip to the base of a square. (See Figure 3-15.)

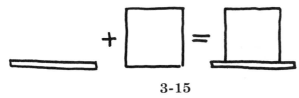

3-15

Add a hatband and a buckle and you have a first-class Pilgrim hat.

lesson 12 **The Christmas Tree**

At Christmas time the teacher's job is not so much to engender interest but to contain it. This is one of those times when the simplest lessons are the best.

you need:

- 12 x 18″ drawing paper
- 10 x 15″ green construction paper

- 6 x 9″ white decoration paper
- 6″ square white present paper (optional)
- pencil, scissors, and paste or glue
- crayons (or other decorating materials)
- and perhaps even a sprinkle of gummed stars

3-16

to present:

1. With the green paper in a vertical position have your class put a dot top center and then draw a line from this dot to each of the two lower corners. Cut on these lines (See Figure 3-16.)   The largest triangle becomes the tree.

2. The tree is to be pasted on the large drawing paper. Once the tree is done have your kids draw, color, and cut out decorations, etc., from the white paper and add presents or whatever else is needed to complete the picture. If you have them, gummed stars are always welcome. (As a matter of fact, your kids probably won't need any advice at all.)

For the More Experienced. Have these classes make a more advanced tree using the folded paper method.

Another popular addition to this lesson is the three-dimensional, wrapped package.

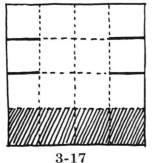

3-17

A Special Gift

1. Have your class fold the 6″ square in sixteen parts as shown on p. 32. Then cut off the shaded portion indicated in Figure 3-17. Cut on the heavy lines, and fold into a box.

2. Once the box is complete, it is to be cut on the side creases as shown in Figure 3-18.

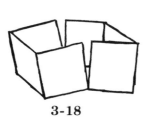

3-18

3-19

3-20

3. The next step is to fold these two half-freed sections into each other to make an enclosed box. Paste. (See Figure 3-19.)

4. Using the green scraps left over from the tree, have your kids cut long strips of ribbon for wrapping the package. A simple paper bow will add a decorative touch. (See Figure 3-20.)

5. Once the package is complete, it can be pasted or glued to the bottom of the picture. (Be sure to allow plenty of time for the paste to dry before displaying the pictures in an upright position.)

lesson 13   **Paper Chains**

The making of paper chains is an activity that is so well-known that I hesitated for a long time before deciding to include it here. I did so because I felt that no honest activity book would be complete without it!

For reasons perhaps no longer perceivable by much of the adult population, children of all ages seem to receive an almost visceral satisfaction in the making of these simple loops. I have seen sixth and seventh graders as engrossed in holiday chain-making as children half their age—so if you are a teacher of older children don't make the mistake of assuming that the joy of chain-making is lost just because some children *look* too old to be chain-makers! If you feel, however, that some of these older children might be a little beyond—or tragically hip and embarrassed by—an activity that they associate with younger children, then you will understand why I have also included instructions for an interlocking chain that the little kids *can't* do!

Simple Pasted Chains

you need:

- paper strips in assorted colors (½ x 6″ or any other convenient size)
- paste or glue

to present:

Simply paste each strip into a loop and link each loop to the preceding one. (See illustration on previous page.)

Interlocking C-Chains (for older kids)

you need:

- 2 x 6″ paper strips in assorted colors
- pencil and scissors

to present:

1. Have your kids fold the paper strip in half widthwise, unfold it (see Figure 3-21A), and then fold the short sides into the center crease. (See Figure 3-21B.) Keeping these last two flaps in position, refold the whole thing on the center fold. (See Figure 3-21C.)

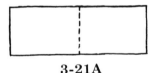
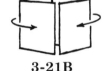

3-21A   3-21B   3-21C

2. With this center fold now at the *left*, have your kids draw a C-shaped figure as illustrated in Figure 3-22. Cut away the shaded areas. Be sure to point out to your kids that they must not cut away all of the center fold— they should retain at least half an inch along the spine of the C.

3-22

3. When cut out and unfolded, the resulting figure resembles a pair of goggles. (See Figure 3-23.)

4. To assemble the chain, fold the first unit to make an O. (See Figure 3-24A.) To make the next link in the chain, loop the second unit through the O. (See Figure 3-24B.) Continue in this fashion until the chain is of desired length! (See Figure 3-24C.)

3-23

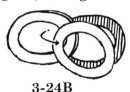
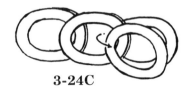

3-24A   3-24B   3-24C

lesson 14 **Santa's Bag of Toys**

Many seeingly complicated constructions lose their mystery when the task is broken down into the most elementary of procedural steps. *Santa's Bag* is a good example of this kind of teaching.

you need:

- 12 x 18″ red construction paper
- 6 x 9″ drawing paper
- pencil, scissors, paste or glue
- string
- paper punch
- crayons (or other decorating materials)

to present:

1. Have your class begin by folding the red paper in half widthwise. (See Figure 3-25A.)

Keeping the paper in this folded position, fold the short sides *in* a distance of approximately 1½″. (See Figure 3-25B.)

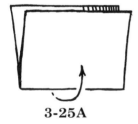

3-25A

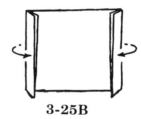

3-25B

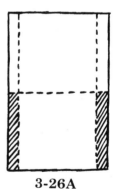

3-26A

2. The paper is then unfolded. Have your kids pencil scribble in the areas indicated in Figure 3-26A. The scribbled areas are then cut away. The bottom flap is once again folded up and the remaining side flaps are pasted down to form the bag.

A hole is then punched in the bag and a string is attached as shown in Figure 3-26B.

3. The 6 x 9″ paper is for drawing and coloring toys and presents to cut out and put in Santa's bag!

3-26B

Santa's Bag of Toys (for the more experienced)

you need:

- 12 x 18″ drawing paper and a smaller piece of same
- 9 x 18″ red paper
- pencil, scissors, paste or glue
- crayons (or other decorating materials)

to present:

1. Turn the 9 x 18″ red paper into a Santa's bag as shown in the previous lesson (but without the punched hole and added string).

2. Have the kids paste the bag on the drawing paper as a "starter" for a picture of their own invention. The smaller piece of drawing paper is used for drawing and coloring toys that can be cut out and placed in the bag.

lesson 15   **The Robots Are Coming**

To make the transition from stick-like "spider" people to more sophisticated figure concepts is *learning*, and as such it cannot be accomplished by force. (By guile, yes, by force—no!) I designed this robot lesson to make the transition between simple geometric drawing and figure drawing a natural progresssion. Thus, from a child's viewpoint the learning is not even noticeable—the lesson is even more fun than recess!

you need:

- practice paper
- 12 x 18″ drawing paper
- crayons (or other decorating materials)

to present:

1. Begin by asking your class if anyone knows what a robot is. (I am sure that at least one person can supply the answer.) Once a satisfactory definition is arrived at, try to give your impersonation of the stiff, slow,

mechanical movements of these ersatz people.* Oh yes, and make a buzzing sound as you go through the motions.

Explain how some robots are controlled by *remote control boxes.* (At this point pick up a chalkboard eraser or any other object that makes a serviceable "remote control box" and continue with your presentation.) A remote control box, you explain, allows the operator to give a command by pressing a button to make the robot respond. Dramatize this by pressing a button on your remote control box and saying, "Robot, turn your head to the right." At that, make a Zzzzzzzzzzzzzzing sound with your mouth and turn *your* head to the right. After giving a few more simple commands, you'll have a whole room full of eager robots-to-be!

Now have your class pretend that *they* are the robots and that *you* are going to be the operator of the remote control box. Give a number of simple commands such as: "Robots, look up (Zzzzzzzzz); robots, look down (Zzzzzzzzz)," etc., and accompany your class in their movements until everyone gets the idea. Once this training session is over, you can have your robots perform all kinds of complex movements including standing up, walking around the room, etc. When they are commanded to return to their Zzzzzzzzzing seats, the next part of the lesson can begin.

In essence, the main body of this lesson is nothing more than a "do as I do" drawing. The kids use their practice papers—you use a sheet of drawing paper taped to the wall. When everyone is ready, begin with your first command: "Robots, draw a medium-sized square near the top of your paper (Zzzzzzzzz).

When done one piece at a time, your robots will end up looking something like Figure 3-27.

Once you and your kids have drawn your practice robot, pass out the drawing paper and let them re-create one of their own and color it. Hair, ears, flashing lights, remote control boxes (and operators), etc. are all imaginative options. (See Figure 3-28.)

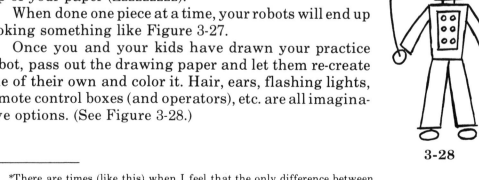

3-27

3-28

---

*There are times (like this) when I feel that the only difference between teaching and show biz is the money!

When they are done, ask your kids to show you where the robot is—"outdoors? indoors? in the classroom? the supermarket? the bedroom?"

I designed the next lesson as a follow-up to this one. For best results have your kids do it soon.

lesson 16   **Statues**

This lesson is the second half of a carefully planned two-part lesson that began with lesson 15, *The Robots Are Coming*. In the first lesson the child was led into seeing the relationship of geometric figures to representational art. In this concluding lesson, the final transition to figure drawing becomes an accomplished reality.

I have done this particular lesson with many grades, but even when it's done with a kindergarten class the results are astonishing!

you need:

- 12 x 18″ drawing paper
- crayons (or other drawing materials)
- and a little bit of courage*

to present:

Begin by placing a table or desk in the front of the room to serve as a model stand, and then tape a 12 x 18″ sheet of drawing paper somewhere in the front of the room for your work-along drawing. Once your props are in order, announce that today you're introducing a new game called *Statues*. Start by choosing a model (let simplicity of dress be your guide here) and position your model on the stand facing the class.

1. The game begins as you draw a "circle-head" high on your drawing paper and instruct your class to do the same. Have your kids complete this head by drawing in

---

*In Chapter 1 I stated that, "This isn't a drawing book ... there isn't a single lesson here that will make you wheel your inadequacies out into the lime light." Although I still plan to follow this rule, you'll have to allow me this one exception! In order to help you help your kids, I want you to draw along. But don't panic—the way that I do it is going to make it easy!

all the details, but at the same time remind them that they are drawing from a real, live statue and therefore they should try to make their drawing look as much as possible like the model. At this point discuss eyes, hair color, etc.

2. Explain that just like the robot of the previous lesson, necks can be added by using a small square. Then, beginning with the shoulder line, have them draw in a rectangle for the body. Discuss shirt or blouse color, and color them. (See Figure 3-29.)

3. For very young groups two rectangles will serve for legs. For slightly older groups I use an inverted V

concept. Feet are smaller rectangles or maybe

just a couple of U's. For skirts, dresses, or shorts, vary the instructions accordingly.

4. Arms are rectangles drawn from the shoulder. Hands can be simple ovals or whatever hand-like shapes your age group can muster.

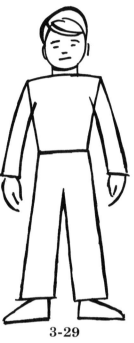

3-29

Further Suggestions: For variations, try a back-view pose. Even though your kids can use both sides of their drawing paper, I would suggest that you have plenty of paper on hand—for a half hour lesson, be prepared to supply at least two sheets per person. (See Figure 3-30.)

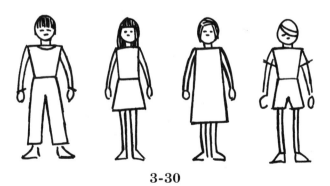

3-30

lesson 17 **Cut-Paper Repeats**

Despite the fact that we live in a culture that associates "cutting paper dolls" with lunacy, kids love to explore the hidden relationships of cut-paper repeats. The inventiveness of these cutouts is enhanced by repetition and limited only by imagination. Cut-paper repeats can become end products in themselves or be transformed into inventive pictures, novelty invitation and greeting cards, or used as a means of decorating almost anything. The only "lunacy" that I have ever seen associated with cut-paper repeats has been in the lack of recognition that has been given this valuable childhood art form!

you need:

- scissors and strips of lightweight paper:
  duplicating or mimeograph paper will work perfectly and if these papers *are* used, the following dimensions will work out nicely:
  for wide repeats—4½ x 11"
  for narrow repeats—2⅛ x 11"

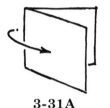

3-31A

to present:

Since all that you are trying to do is introduce a concept, your instruction period normally ends the moment the concept is understood.

The basic folding can be done in a number of ways but I think that the following set of instructions is as good as any:

The Two-Fold Unit. Fold the strip in half widthwise and then fold it in half again. (See Figures 3-31A and 3-31B.)

3-31B

The Three-Fold Unit. The Three-Fold Unit is nothing more than the Two-Fold Unit folded once again. (See Figure 3-32.)

3-32

The basic idea, of course, is to plan a design that will retain enough of each of the folded edges so that it will not fall apart when opened. Once the drawing is complete, the part of the folded paper packet which is not part of the design is then cut away.

Using the Two-Fold Unit. The two activities presented in Figures 3-33A and 3-33B are perfect end-products for the very young (and good concept examples for older children). They are both done using the wide strip.

The first example can be turned into anything from ghosts to angels to girls in nightgowns as in Figure 3-34A. The row of houses can be decorated in many ways or even

3-33A

3-33B

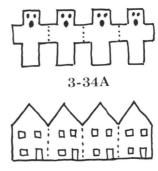

3-34A

3-34B

pasted to a larger sheet of paper and used as a "starter" for a residential street scene. (See Figure 3-34B.)

Advanced Two-Fold Units. Once kids understand that the success of the repeats depends upon leaving some paper intact at the folds, all kinds of great things can happen. Here are dogs and frogs done using narrow paper. (See Figures 3-35A and 3-35B.)

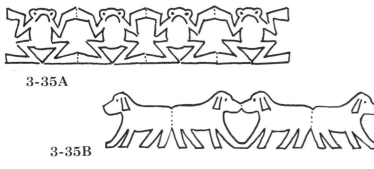

3-35A

3-35B

Advanced Three-Fold Units (wide strip). And finally, for those who understand the basic complexities of cut paper, the whole project can be approached from the viewpoint of the half-drawings of folded paper symmetry (p. 33) as in Figure 3-36.

3-36

Further Suggestions: The very creative may want to explore vertical repeats like these acrobats in Figure 3-37 which were done using narrow paper in a Two-Fold Unit.

3-37

lesson 18 **"Snowflakes," etc.**

The cut-paper repeats of the previous lesson make a good introduction to these somewhat more elaborate cutting and folding activities.

you need:

- square sheets of lightweight paper (duplicating or mimeograph paper will do fine)
- scissors

to present:

"Snowflakes" for the Very Young

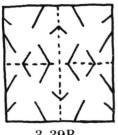

3-38A

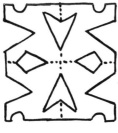

3-38B

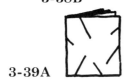

3-39A

3-39B

Although all real snowflakes have six points, paper "snowflakes" can have any number of points, for the fun of making "snowflakes" has nothing to do with reality. As a matter of fact, by fairly realistic standards, a "snowflake" for the very young may not even have any points at all!

The paper is folded in half and then in half again as shown in Figures 3-38A and 3-38B. Pieces are clipped out of the edges of the folded packet and then the paper is unfolded to reveal a decorative repeat design.

The folding and the unfolding is easy—it is the *cutting* that will present problems for the very young. Here are conceptual problems that will cause their share of consternation:

Cutting vs. Cutting Out. Just because *you* understand the difference between cutting and cutting out doesn't mean that *they* do. There will be those who will diligently make all kinds of cuts and not understand why the unfolded "snowflake" is such a flop. (See Figures 3-39A and 3-39B.) To help kids overcome this problem you will have to show them personally how to snip out the little pie-shaped pieces. The problem is generally not so much one of cutting but of concept, for it is not until they begin to focus their attention on the snipped-out pieces that progress can be made.

The Problem of the Unretained Edge. Another problem that may arise will be some child's failure to understand that the folds have a structural relationship to the finished snowflake. "Cut a piece, skip a piece" is the singsong rule to be learned here. (See Figure 3-40.)

Folding Variations. Rather than folding the square as described on the previous page, try having your class fold their squares on the diagonal and then fold the two opposing corners so that they overlap each other. (See Figures 3-41A and 3-41B.) Pieces are then cut away in the usual fashion.

3-40

"Snowflakes" for the More Experienced

Begin by having your class fold a six-pointed star as found on page 162. Since snowflakes cut from this star fold have six points, they more closely resemble the real thing. Remembering that you had read somewhere that no two snowflakes are ever the same is as good a conversational springboard as any to invent some really wild creations such as Figure 3-42. So, once your class gets the idea—stand back and let it snow!

3-41A   3-41B

3-42

lesson 19   **Star Clowns**

Star-people are fun to make and one of the easiest is the clown!

you need:

3-43

- a square sheet of drawing paper (6″ or 9″ squares will do fine)
- pencil, scissors and crayons (or other decorating materials)

to present:

1. Have your class draw a five-pointed star on the square paper. (See *Full-Paper Stars*, p. 48.) Cut away shaded portions. (See Figure 3-43.)

2. Using crayons (or other decorating materials), have your kids add face and hat, clothes, shoes, hands, etc. (See lead examples.)

Further Suggestions: Have your kids fold the clown figures to make knees bend, feet stick out, etc.

For a slightly more advanced star-figure see *New Year's Baby*, p. 168.

lesson 20   # The World's Easiest Weaving

Weaving has always been a difficult concept to introduce to the very young—but no longer! If you have ever tried teaching the fundamentals of weaving to young children, you will be the first to agree that this is truly the world's easiest weaving lesson.

Weaving for the Very Young

you need:

- construction paper in the following colors and sizes:
    - 12 x 18″ base paper (any color)
    - 3 x 18″ strips of dark-colored paper (two each)
    - 3 x 18″ strips of light-colored paper (two each)
    - 2 x 12″ strips of white paper (eight each)
- stapler, and paste or glue

to present:

1. Each weaving unit must be assembled with the help of a stapler. Staple the four alternating strips of 3 x 18″ paper to the base paper as shown in Figure 3-44. These long strips become the *warp* of our weaving.

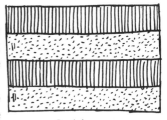

3-44

2. To operate the loom, simply instruct your class to "pick up both light-colored strips and hold them in one hand." At that point they are to push in the white horizontal strip, the *woof*, with the other hand. (See lead illustration.)

3. Once the horizontal strip is in place, have your class drop the light-colored strips, pick up the two dark-colored strips, and push in a new white horizontal strip. This alternating two-step process is continued until the weaving is complete. Staple the last two ends of the warp and have the kids paste down any loose flaps. And that's that! (See Figure 3-45.)

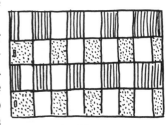

3-45

Weaving for the More Experienced

Using the same approach to weaving as in *Weaving for the Very Young*, all kinds of interesting effects are possible.

you need:

- construction paper in the following colors and sizes:
    - 12 x 18″ base paper (any color)
    - 2 x 18″ colored strips
    - 2 x 12″ strips of white paper
- stapler, and paste or glue.

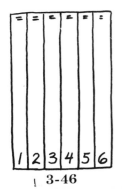

3-46

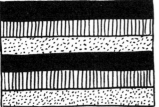

3-47A

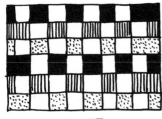

3-47B

to present:

Odd and Even Weaving. For this activity staple six 2 x 18″ strips—all of the same color—to the base paper, as in the previous lesson, and number each strip consecutively from one to six. (See Figure 3-46.)

Proceed with the weaving as before but this time, rather than the kids picking up light strips and then dark strips, have them pick up first the odd and then the even-numbered strips! The final results will be an all-over checkerboard effect.

Odd and Even Color Circle Weaving. For this activity the six 2 x 18″ strips are all color-related. These long strips are chosen from an analogous color scheme (see p. 59). Using yellow, green, and blue, for example, the loom would be set in just that order: Y–G–B–Y–G–B. (See Figure 3-47A.) Once the long strips have been stapled into position, number them as in *Odd and Even Weaving.* Then, using the white strips in the usual way, weave accordingly. The results will be a surprisingly intricate and colorful repeat pattern! (See Figure 3-47B.)

lesson 21   **Two-Handed Drawing**

Like many other good basic lessons, this activity works just as well with older kids as it does with younger ones.

you need:

- 12 x 18″ drawing paper
- chalk and chalkboard
- tape
- crayons (or other decorating materials)

to present:

1. I like to begin this lesson in the air. I ask the class to hold up their hands as I challenge them to try to duplicate my airbound hand movements. Each hand movement that I make is nothing more than a "mirror image" of the other. (See Figures 3-48A, 3-48B and 3-48C.)

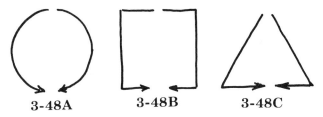

3-48A   3-48B   3-48C

Your class should have no great problem doing and identifying a circle, square, and triangle as "drawn " in air.

2. Following the "air" exercises, two-handed chalkboard drawings are a natural. I begin by drawing some kind of a two-handed drawing on the board and then asking for volunteers to re-create my drawings. Once they get the idea, I ask for volunteers to do some creative two-handed chalkboard work.

3. After everyone understands the nature of the problem, I have each child choose two crayons while I tape their drawing paper to their working surfaces. At that point I put them all to work creating their own two-handed designs. The finished designs are then colored to make a complete presentation.

lesson 22 A Thousand Hearts

hol·i·day 1. *a day appointed by law for suspension of business in commemoration of some event.* No matter what the dictionary says, for kids this just ain't so, for in their world holidays have nothing to do with business or suspension of business. It has to do with *fun.* Ask children to name their favorite holidays and the tally will be an overwhelming vote for "Christmas, Halloween, and Valentine's Day!"

Learning to Make Hearts

you need:
- paper
- pencils
- scissors

3-49A   3-49B

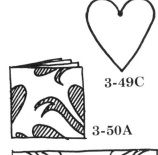

3-49C

3-50A

3-50B

to present:

For the very young, hearts are not easy to make. Here are a few ideas that can help your kids overcome this difficulty.

V Hearts. This is the easiest method I know to teach children how to draw hearts. I begin by having the class draw a V (see Figure 3-49A) followed by a dot placed midway between the forked ends of the V. (See Figure 3-49B.) With a "hill" connecting the dot to each of the V tops, the heart is complete. (See Figure 3-49C.) It may not be the best heart in the world, but for a little kid it sure is a good beginning!

Folded Paper Hearts. The second easiest method (although this isn't for the very, very young) is the folded paper method. (See p. 34.)

Valentine Lace. Once the concept of the folded heart is understood, try having your class incorporate hearts into their folded paper "snowflakes" (p. 98) to create an exciting Valentine Lace. Figure 3-50A shows a paper folded into quarters (the shaded portions to be removed), and Figure 3-50B shows the same paper opened to expose the "lace." For best results your class should be encouraged to include not only hearts but other gracefully shaped cutouts in the designing of their lace.

Your Basic Valentine

One form or another of the following valentine can be used succcessfully with *any* age group.

you need:

- 9 x 6″ white drawing or construction paper
- 6 x 4½″ lightweight white paper
- 6 x 4½″ red paper (two each)
- scissors, and paste or glue

to present:

1. Have the 9 x 6″ white paper folded widthwise to make a "book."
2. Using the other sheet of white paper, have your

class prepare a Valentine Lace according to the instructions above. Paste this lace on one of the sheets of red paper and then paste this lace-on-red to the front of the folded white paper (from step 1).

3. Use the remaining red paper to cut out a heart to paste on the inside of the card.

Suggestions: All kinds of variations are possible here. For some classes you might want to add a red heart to the cover, or a smaller white heart to paste on top of the inside heart. Another valentine that is always popular is one that uses the paper spring (see p. 44) to make the inside heart pop out when the card is opened. And of course, your kids will have plenty of ideas of their own!

lesson 23 Magic Reruns

A child's first encounter with "carbon" paper is always fun to watch, for in young minds this transfer of images is nothing less than miraculous!

Magic Reruns for the Very Young

you need:
- 6 x 9" and 6 x 4½" drawing paper
- pencil and crayons

to present:

1. Have your kids color one side of the 6 x 4½" paper with a heavy coating of black (or some other dark-colored) crayon.

2. The larger paper is to be folded widthwise to make a "book."

3. When they are ready, have your kids place the smaller paper crayoned side down between the "pages" of the folded "book." Tell your class to draw a picture or a design on the front cover of their "book"—with a pencil—and when using their pencils, to "press down hard."

Once they open their books and discover the transferred image, excitement will run high! Suggest that they color *both* pictures.

Further Comments: Your kids will be both delighted and baffled with these *Magic Reruns.* Some of your kids, naturally, will put in their carbons wrong side up and will share this discovery with those around them. Others will try color teleportation experiments by drawing with colored crayon to see if color as well as line can be sent by magic.

Since the paper is already folded, Magic Reruns are a natural for greeting cards.

Rainbow Reruns

Whereas the Magic Reruns is a lesson designed for the very young, I guarantee that you will find Rainbow Reruns to be a popular activity with kids of *all* ages!

you need:

- small sheets of drawing paper (3 x 4½″ or any other convenient size)
- pencils and crayons

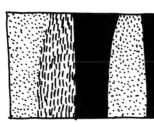

3-51

to present:

1. Have your kids color one of the small sheets with a heavy layer of crayon. They should be encouraged to alternate colors freely as suggested in Figure 3-51.

2. Once the "rainbow" sheet is complete, have your kids place another sheet of drawing paper on top of their "rainbow" sheet and —using a pencil—make a drawing on this top sheet. (See Figure 3-52.)

3. When the drawing is finished, have your kids pick up the top sheet, turn it over, and *presto!*—a whimsical "rainbow-colored" picture is the result! (See Figure 3-53.)

3-52

3-53

Further Suggestions: This is a great activity that takes to all kinds of experimentation.

One of the first discoveries that your class will make is that the *Rainbow Reruns* come out backwards! For those who want to use lettering, this poses all kinds of challenges! You might suggest that they write what they want written on another piece of paper, reverse it, and hold it up to a window to copy the reverse lettering as it is seen through the paper. This backwards lettering can then be used as a model for the "good" one.

For some reason or other when kids begin this activity they seem to work completely with *line* drawings. Once things are moving well, suggest to your class that they can also use their pencil for coloring in *areas!*

And finally—try using these Rainbow Reruns to decorate greeting cards. They're beautiful!

lesson 24   **Smile!**

As an experienced teacher of art activities, I know how hard it is to try to predict the outcome of a lesson just by reading about it. For example: this lesson (especially in its primary form) does not look particularly exciting. What kid would want a camera that only has three sides? And yet—this primary camera is always one of the most popular lessons of the year! Kids are always asking to "do it again." Why? I don't know. I guess you would have to be a child to understand.

A Camera for the Very Young

you need:

- 9″ square of black construction paper
- 3 x 18″ strip of drawing paper
- 1 x 2″ piece of white paper
- stapler, and paste or glue
- crayons (or other decorating materials)

to present:

1. Have your class begin by dividing the 18″ strip into photograph-size divisions. In each section have them

3-54

draw a different head (boy's head, girl's head, clown's head, horse's head, etc.) as shown in Figure 3-54.

2. Fold the 9″ square into four parts as shown in Figure 3-55A and cut on the heavy lines. Fold so that Flap 4 lies on top of Flap 3 and then staple this assembly into a three-sided box. When positioning this staple, try to keep it centered and towards the back as indicated in Figure 3-55B. Fold down the inside flap to make a "film compartment." (See Figure 3-55C.)

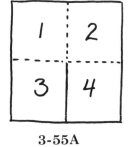

3-55A

3-55B

3-55C

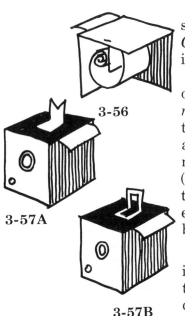

3-56

3-57A

3-57B

3. You should then take each child's completed film strip and draw it across a table edge (see *Table-Edge Curls*, p. 45) to make a film roll. The film roll is then inserted into the camera housing as shown in Figure 3-56.

4. For a final touch of realism have your kids use one of the small white papers to cut out a *lens* and a *shutter release* (or "pressing button"). These are to be pasted to the front of their cameras as in Figure 3-57A. From another of the small pieces of white paper have them make a *view finder* and paste it to the top of the camera. (See Figure 3-57B.) An easy way to make a view finder is to fold a 1 x 2″ white paper widthwise, cut a notch at one end, and paste! For slightly older children, a folded paper buckle-style view finder will offer a little more challenge.

Operating Instructions: Children take great glee in pointing these cameras at others, saying "Smile" and tearing off the first picture that extends beyond the camera housing—new pictures being torn off as they are needed. Be sure to keep plenty of blank film strips on hand.

A Camera for the More Experienced

you need:

- 12″ square and 11½″ square of black construction paper
- 18 x 2¾″ strip of drawing paper
- 1 x 2″ pieces of white paper
- stapler, and paste or glue
- crayons (or other decorating materials)

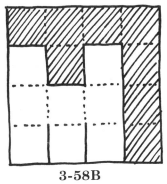

to present:

1. Have your class fold both of the large squares into sixteen parts. The 12″ square is trimmed and cut as illustrated in Figure 3-58A; the 11½″ square as illustrated in Figure 3-58B.* Both papers are then folded and pasted into boxes.

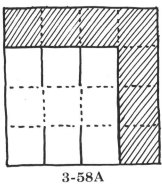

3-58A   3-58B

2. Prepare your film strip as described in the previous lesson (see *A Camera for the Very Young*). The film is placed in the smaller box and the outside end of the roll is pushed through the forward slot as shown in Figure 3-59. This smaller box is then fitted into the larger camera housing box.

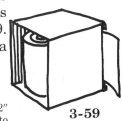

3-59

---

*Occasionally an exceptionally bright child will ask why we need a 12″ square sheet of paper to make a 9″ square. The answer of course is obvious to anyone who has ever worked with large numbers of children: an art activity bogs down in such joyless activities as trying to use a ruler to divide a 9″ square into thirds!

Super-Dooper Flash Attachment

If you really want to have the best, this Super-Dooper Flash Attachment is a must!

you need:

- 6 x 4½″ black construction paper
- 4½ x 6″ white drawing or construction paper
- 4¼″ circle pattern and a 2″ circle pattern
- stapler, and paste or glue

to present:

1. To make the upright part of your flash units, staple the black paper to the outside camera housing as shown in Figure 3-60A below. Once anchored, the black paper is rolled up and stapled into a cylinder as shown in Figure 3-60B. Finally, the excess unrolled paper is trimmed away as shown in Figure 3-60C.

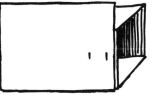  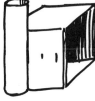

3-60A   **3-60B**   **3-60C**

2. To make the reflector and flash bulb, have your kids trace the larger circle on the white paper and then cut it out. The smaller circle pattern is then traced onto the middle of the larger white circle. This last circle line must then be scored (see p. 61). Cut on the heavy lines. (See Figure 3-61.)

3-61

3. The reflector and flashbulb unit is folded on the scored lines as illustrated in Figure 3-62 and pasted into its final form. Staple the reflector to the upright cylinder and your camera is ready for action!

3-62

lesson 25 **Gretchen's Magic Transfer**

In our house, sunless Sunday afternoons are the time that the kids and I gather around the family table with paste, pencils, scissors and crayons to see what we can make, discover, or invent. Here is the result of one memorable afternoon that made me quickly revise the following week's lesson plans for *all* of my classes!

you need:

- 9 x 12″ drawing paper
- pencil and white crayons
- any hard smooth instrument (see below)
- drawings, cartoons, and photographs snipped from newspapers and comic books (or anything printed on common newsprint)

to present:

First of all, let me explain what this lesson is all about. For some reason or other anything printed on newsprint can be easily transferred to paper which has been coated with a layer of white crayon. Rubbing with concentrated pressure accomplishes this transfer. The transfer will take place whether (1) one rubs the back of the image to be transferred, or (2) the back of the paper that the image is to be transferred on. In my experience the first method works better with younger children, the second with older children.

Applying the pressure that makes the transfer possible can be done in a number of different ways. Here are two (see Figures 3-63A and 3-63B):

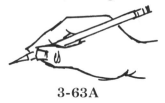

3-63A

Using the rounded point of a pencil

3-63B

Using a scissor handle held in this position

Magic Transfers for the Very Young

1. Begin by having your class draw an outline of a large house but explain that it must be drawn *without* windows and doors.

2. When they are done, have them choose a drawing, cartoon, or photograph from an assortment that you have snipped from newspapers and comic books (because of the color, comic books and Sunday funnies have a special appeal). After they have made their choice, have them place their newsprint picture on their drawn house wherever they feel a window should be. Then, in preparation for the next step, they are to trace around this picture with a pencil. This pencil line becomes the outline of the first window.

3. Have your kids color in this window area with a white crayon. Then have them turn the newsprint picture face down over the crayoned window area and rub over the back of the newsprint clipping with a hard, smooth instrument. Lift the newsprint and *presto!*—the window is filled with an instant picture. That's window one. Now that they have the idea, let them continue at their own speed.

Magic Transfers for the More Experienced

The only additional information needed here concerns newsprint, which has a tendency to tear under the pressure applied by older children. Therefore, these kids will be happier (1) drawing their picture, (2) holding their drawn picture to the light, and (3) on the *back* of this picture, penciling a line around those areas in which a magic transfer is planned.

The activity then proceeds in the same way except that the transfer is made by laying the drawn picture on top of the newsprint picture and making the transfer by rubbing the area on the back that was previously outlined in pencil.

Picture Suggestions. Interior scenes are fun. Try using the transfers for the pictures on the wall or for the picture screen on a television set. Automobiles, etc., allow for some funny scenes, with people of all sizes peering out of the windows. Movie theaters or billboards also work well. Another very popular idea is to draw people in T-shirts, etc., and use the transfers to decorate the fronts!

Final Comment: Remember, of course, that all transfers will appear in reverse. This is important where lettering might appear. (Since the transfer is actually on *top* of the coating of white crayon, unwanted lettering can be quickly removed by simply scraping it off.)

lesson 26   Camping Out

Stand-ups are always fun to do. Although Camping Out is one of the easiest to make, you'll soon discover why its appeal is not limited to any one age group!

you need:

- construction paper in the following colors and sizes:
    - 12″ green square
    - 12 x 6″ water blue
    - 12 x 4½″ tent-colored paper
    - smaller pieces of green for brushes, etc.
- white or manila drawing paper for people, etc.

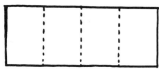

3-64A

• scissors, and paste or glue

• crayons (or other decorating materials)

to present:

1. Have your class cut one side of the water paper to make a more realistic-looking "shoreline," or have them use the water paper to make a brook.

2. The tent is made by folding the 12 x 4½" paper into quarters and folding it up as shown in Figures 3-64A and 3-64B.

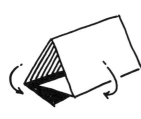

3-64B

3. Small stand-ups can be made by bending back a "pasting foot." (See Figure 3-65.) In the lead illustration, the fire and the small bushes have been made in this way.

4. Taller objects like the pine tree are best made by using both vertical *and* horizontal folds. Figures 3-66A and 3-66B should be self-explanatory.

3-65

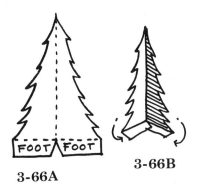

3-66A

3-66B

5. Encourage your class to add anything else that they feel is needed, which might include people, sleeping bags, animals, turtles, fish, and perhaps even an island connected to the mainland by a bridge!

4

To The Walls !

Without art, the world would be a dreary place! Consider the change that a few picutres can make in brightening up a room, or what happens in September when the school corridors suddenly bloom in childhood art.

Some school children need little or no creative encouragement to decorate the walls, but there are others who need all the help they can get just to get started. Too much direction and creativity is stifled—too little, and it may never awaken at all! To supply this balance is the goal of every well prepared art lesson.

One way to do this is to use "starters"—lessons designed to distract the child from his inhibitions long enough to allow his creative energies to surface and express themselves with all the vigor and individuality of life itself. This, then, is a chapter of "starters."

Furthermore, as the title suggests, each of these "starter" lessons has been chosen for its decorative qualities—so call in your kids and let's see what we can do about brightening up your school!

lesson 1   **Pointillism**

Like most creative people I take great pride in presenting an original art lesson, but there are other times when I take an equal amount of pride in my ability to recognize a good lesson when I see one. This lesson I borrowed from Georges Seurat (1859-91)—it was one of his best!

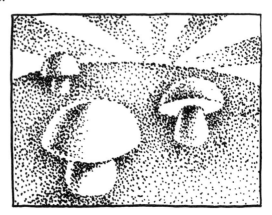

you need:

- 6 x 4½″ white drawing paper
- crayons or, better still, fine-line markers (if you have them)

to present:

Most people think of *Pointillism* as being pictures done with little dots. Although this definition is harmless enough for most purposes, I would advise the classroom teacher to avoid the word "dot" completely. Dot-making is to be discouraged not because it raises the noise level (which it does) but because it destroys the points of crayons and markers and gives nothing in exchange. Instead—have your kids use *short dashes*. Superficially they look like dots, but they contain the decided vitality that makes this activity a success.

1. Have your kids lightly pencil in whatever picture idea they choose.

2. Once the picture is penciled in, explain how the short dashes are to be used and encourage intermixing different colors of dashes to produce intermediate hues.

Further Suggestions: If you will take the time to show your class a painting or two by Seurat (a library book will do fine), you'll send your activity off to a flying start.

The finished pictures take on an added magnificence when mounted on a 5 x 6½" dark cuff set against a 9 x 12" light background. (See p. 256 for framing instructions and terminology.)

lesson 2   **Stencil Trees**

Stencil art can be as boring as an unvaried diet but, at its best, can be as exciting as an unopened birthday package! This particular lesson is not only creative and decorative, but has that added note of surprise that makes it come forth with a strutting life and vitality all its own.

you need:

- plenty of 3 x 2¼" (approximate size*) drawing or construction paper
- 9 x 12" drawing paper
- scissors (preferably pointed or semi-pointed)
- pencil and crayons (or other decorating materials)

---

*From time to time I feel that it is necessary to remind you that most of my fractional measurements are standardized to leave usable remainders.

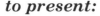

to present:

Kids like surprises so indulge them by beginning this leson with a little misdirection:

1. Have your kids draw a potato shape on one of the small papers in such a way so that the shape does not touch any of the borders of the paper. Cut away the shaded area and save the paper that it was drawn on. (See Figure 4-1.)

4-1

2. This second step will go more slowly since some of your kids may have a little difficulty drawing a leafless tree. (Like the "potato," the tree should not touch the borders of the paper.) When done, have your kids cut away the tree and save the paper it was drawn on. (See Figure 4-2.)

3. NOW—the fun begins. Show your kids how to use the "potato" stencil by coloring *inward* towards the center of the stencil with a green crayon. (Color *outward* and the stencil may tear.) Each time the kids stencil their "potato" have them then turn their stencil at another angle and use it again elsewhere on their paper. In Figure 4-3 the same "potato" was used three times and in three different positions.

4-2

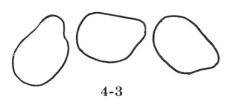

4-3

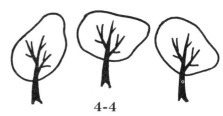

4-4

4. Placing the tree stencil so that it overlaps the "potato," have your kids stencil in the tree shape with a black crayon.* Figure 4-4 is a continuation of the "potato" picture begun in step 3.

5. From here on the picture idea is turned over to the kids. Let them exchange their stencils freely and make more if they so desire. In a hill picture (as illustrated at the

---

*Expect to get a few complaints here. For some reason or other, most kids want to make their tree trunks *brown*. This is a good opportunity to have the class do a little research on tree color. Maybe even you will be surprised!

top of the previous page), the green trees would nearly disappear against the green hill. In cases like these, recommend yellow-green for the grass.

lesson 3   Line Games

We have all known activities that began with great promise and then slowly sputtered to a weak conclusion. These Line Games are just the opposite—they start weak, gain in strength as the period develops, and finish with all the gusto of a polished performance. Your kids will love them.

you need:

- paper (duplicating or mimeograph paper will work fine)
- pencils, crayons, pens, or fine-line markers (preferably the last if you have them)

Game 1—Good Vibrations

to present:

1. Have your kids place their paper in a horizontal position and then draw a wavy line across the paper. At the bottom of each "valley" have them place a *very small* dot. (See Figure 4-5.)
2. Then announce the rules of this "game": they are to draw more wavy lines, but all lines must run reasonably parallel until they reach the dots. At each of

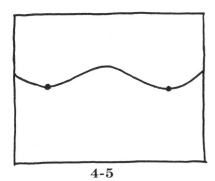

4-5

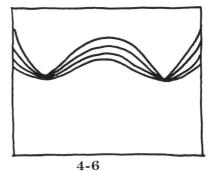

4-6

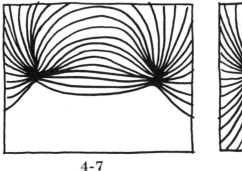

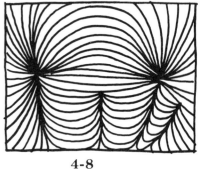

4-7   4-8

these dots or "kissing points" the lines must briefly touch before continuing their journey. (See Figure 4-6.)

3. When the upper part of the paper has been completed, the lower half of the paper is done in the same way, using the same "kissing points." (See Figure 4-7.)

Further Suggestions: Some of the most interesting creations appear when new "kissing points" are added (or deleted) as the picture develops. Figure 4-8 shows what happens when new "kissing points" are introduced.

As a rule, the closer the lines, the better the results.

Game 2—Wipeout

In many ways this game resembles Good Vibrations but this variation is played with obstacles!

1. Have your kids place their paper in a horizontal position and then choose some kind of a motif as their theme. Whatever the motif, it should be varied in size for added interest. (See Figure 4-9.)

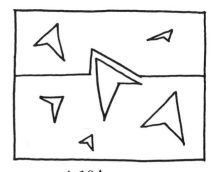

4-9   4-10A

4-10B   4-10C

2. Explain to your class that each line must travel a straight course until it meets with an obstacle. At that point the line must go around the obstacle before continuing again *on the same original course.* Figures 4-10A, 4-10B and 4-10C below will explain the process better than words. The lower half of the picture is completed in the same way.

3. Unlike the first line game, the player sometimes finds himself faced with a pocket that allows no escape. The area in Figure 4-11 identified by a question mark is a case in point. If the artist player enters this pocket there would be no room left for escape, therefore the player must continue on leaving the pocket untouched. Later the player returns to the pocket to finish it off in the manner of a self-contained tide pool. (See Figures 4-12A and 4-12B.)

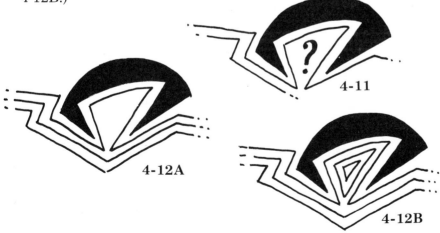

4-11

4-12A

4-12B

Further Suggestions: For added variety: (1) have the first line start at the left but travel off the bottom of paper (see Figure 4-13A), (2) have the first line start from

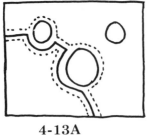
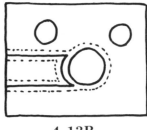
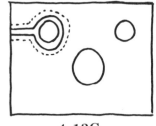

4-13A   4-13B   4-13C

began (see Figure 4-13B), or (3) have the first line encompass a single object as its starting point (see Figure 4-13C). (Dotted lines represent the path of subsequent lines.)

lesson 4   Advanced Silhouettes

If your class enjoys making silhouettes, then the fun has just begun!

Black, White, and Gray

you need:

- 9 x 12″ black, white, and gray construction paper and extra scraps of the same colors as needed
- pencil, scissors, paste or glue

to present:

1. The best way to present this lesson is simply to show your class a few examples. If you are too timid to paste up an example or two of your own, then hold up this book so that your kids can see Figures 4-14A and 4-14B.

2. Explain to your kids that this lesson is really no more difficult than a black and white silhouette activity, perhaps even easier because you have one more shade to work with. Review with your class the basic concepts of the silhouette (pp. 56-57) and let them get started whenever they are ready by choosing one paper for the background sheet and cutting and pasting the others as needed.

4-14A

4-14B

Further Suggestions: If you stock more than one shade of grey, the possibilities become even more exciting.

Silhouettes in Bloom

you need:

- three or more sheets of 9 x 12″ construction paper, all of which are tints and shades of the same color (for example: dark red, red, and pink; or dark green, green, and light green)
- pencils, scissors, paste or glue

to present:

This lesson is done in exactly the same way as the preceding lesson but for some reason kids find it harder to do. They have difficulty understanding how a picture can have any kind of validity when it is done in only one color. ("Who ever heard of a green sky?") But when they get started, this activity is literally a prize-winner.

Further Suggestions: For an even greater treat, try three shades of one color *plus* black and white.

lesson 5 **Woven Pictures**

To have survived as an art form for the last two hundred years, the silhouette must have some kind of basic appeal. Combine the silhouette concept with weaving and you have doubled the basic interest. This activity does just that.

you need:

- construction paper in the following colors:
  one white, one light color, and one dark color
- pencil, and ruler or straightedge
- scissors, and paste or glue

to present:

1. Using the *Basic Weaving* instructions on p. 66, have your class weave a mat using the white and the light-colored construction paper.

2. The dark paper is used to make a silhouette overlay in one of the following ways. (See Figures 4-15A and 4-15B):

By using the dark paper to make a positive shape*

By using the dark paper to make a negative shape*

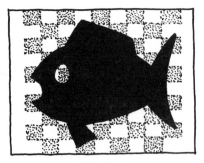

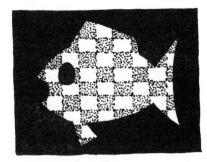

4-15A

4-15B

*See discussion of positive and negative shapes on p. 55.

Either way, paste down the dark paper and your woven pictures are complete.

lesson 6 **Martian Texture Hunt**

In the first chapter of this book I recommended saving all the odds and ends of old crayons. This lesson is one of the reasons why.

you need:

- two sheets of drawing paper
- broken pieces of peeled crayons

to present:

1. With a light pencil line have your kids compose a "Martian" scene in which *nothing* is recognizable except maybe land and sky (and even that could be quicksand and vapor or mud). In order to get the best possible design, tell them that they must have some large objects, some medium-sized objects, and at least one object that appears to extend beyond the limits of the picture. (See Figure 4-16.)

2. Once the picture is sketched out, have your kids take the peeled crayons and the other piece of drawing paper and prowl the room to look for textures. Once they find a promising texture they are to place their "practice" paper over it and make a sample rubbing with the side of a peeled crayon. (See Figure 4-17.) Once they have a sheet full of practice rubbings, let them use their new found knowledge in applying textures to their Martian landscape.

4-16

4-17

For other *Crayon Rubbing* activities see pp. 80 and 134.

lesson 7 **Winter Reflections**

I have always had a love affair with crayons. I like the way they look, the way they feel, and like many kids I never open a new box of crayons without smelling them. But best of all I like the things that crayons can *do*. This lesson uses crayons in an uncommon way.

you need:

- 12 x 18″ white drawing paper
- crayons

to present:

1. The paper is first folded in half lengthwise. Announce that today's lesson is an ice picture and that everyone in this picture will be skating, falling, slipping, or sliding *on or slightly above the folded line*. Tell them to color in their figures but not to add background, as that will be added later. (See Figure 4-18.)

4-18

2. Once the figures are done, have your kids refold the picture on the center line in such a way as to have the picture on the inside of the top part of the fold. With the handle of a scissor (or any other hard, smooth object) rub the back of the crayoned figures. (See Figure 4-19.) When the rubbing is complete, have your kids reopen the folded paper to discover the icy reflections! From this point on, the picture is "finished" by adding in anything that is needed to make this a completed winter scene.

Further Suggestions: The rubbing sometimes removes some of the surface of the original picture but that can be easily touched up. The reflections are best and most convincing when they are left untouched.

4-19

lesson 8   Ricochet Lines

I don't know how to classify this lesson. I discovered this idea in a science book but if this is science it is not science as most of us think of it! Here it is in its most basic form.

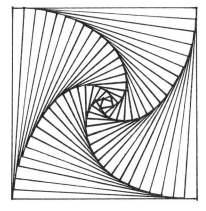

you need:

- any size paper
- a ruler or straightedge
- pencil, pen, or fine-line marker

to present:

1. Begin by having your kids draw (or trace) a square (any size). From this point on you wil have to work along with them. For demonstration purposes, use either a chalkboard or a large piece of paper taped to the wall for your "do as I do" drawing. (See Figures 4-20A, 4-20B and 4-20C.)

The basic idea (as demonstrated above) is not as

4-20A

4-20B

4-20C

difficult as it looks. It is simply a matter of drawing each line so that it misses the oncoming corner. Incidentally, the closer together the lines, the better the results. Once your kids get the idea, let them proceed at their own speed.

2. The clockwise figure in step 1 becomes the design shown in the lead illustration. These figures can also be done counterclockwise. Figure 4-21 is what happens when you put the two together:

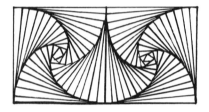

4-21

Suggestions: Ricochet Lines can be arranged and rearranged to make a number of fascinating designs. And when color is added—wow!

lesson 9   **Patterned for Fun**

If *Ricochet Lines* is a mechanically determined design, this two-part lesson is just the opposite. Here—all of the patterns are invented, and the results are fascinating!

you need:

- 9 x 12″ drawing paper
- pencil and crayons (or other fine-line drawing instruments)

Patterned for Fun—1

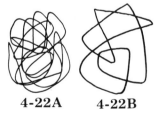

4-22A   **4-22B**

to present:

1. Begin by showing your class the two basic types of scribbles: (1) the "tangled" scribble (see Figure 4-22A), and (2) the "open" scribble (see Figure 4-22B). Explain that in today's activity only a large "open" scribble will work.

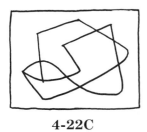

4-22C

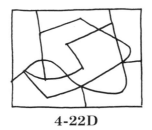

4-22D

2. Once they have used their pencils to draw a large, open scribble, have them add a few additional outside lines so that the whole paper is divided into compartments. (See Figures 4-22C and 4-22D.)

3. Next—explain that today the crayons will be used for drawing lines and, furthermore, that these lines will be arranged to create *patterns*. At this point take time out to demonstrate a few line patterns such as those in Figures 4-23A, 4-23B and 4-23C.

4. When everyone has the idea, explain that each of the compartments of the scribbled sheet are to be patterned in a different way.

5. And finally, when they are done, have them outline the compartment boundaries with a black crayon as shown in the lead illustration.

4-23A

4-23B

4-23C

Patterned for Fun—2

Although this lesson is a follow-up to the previous lesson, allow a few days to a week to elapse before trying this second part. With that, the trap is set!

1. Without mentioning that this lesson is in any way related to the previous lesson, begin by asking your class to lightly pencil in a picture idea in outline form. Insist that the drawing be large and without a lot of small detail.

2. THEN—when the drawings are ready and waitting, spring your announcement that this is a follow-up lesson and that they are going to use their crayons—not for coloring—but for *pattern*. This time, however, suggest that they simplify their line pattern. Suggest some of the following time-honored techniques (see Figures 4-24A, 4-24B and 4-24C):

When they get the idea—put them to work! (See Figures 4-25A and 4-25B.)

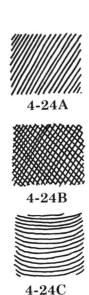

4-24A

4-24B

4-24C

4-25A

4-25B

lesson 10   **Pipe Dreams**

If I were you and you were me, I would probably be accusing you of padding this book with a lesson called Pipe Dreams. How could one be naive enough to believe that anyone could make a successful lesson out of a lot of pipes? Frankly—I wouldn't have believed it myself if I hadn't stumbled on this lesson by accident! Older kids, particularly, love it.

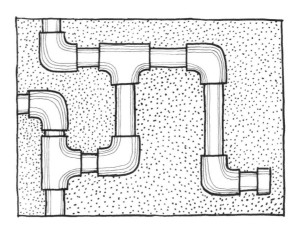

you need:

- light gray, light green, light blue, or any other 9 x 12″ construction paper that is subdued in color
- a *regular* pencil and a *white* pencil (or, if necessary, white chalk)

to present:

1. Show your class how to draw the basic plumbing fittings (see Figure 4-26):

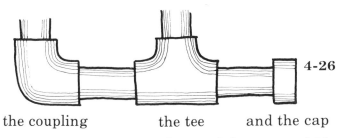

the coupling   the tee   and the cap   4-26

2. Once the fittings are understood, have your kids pencil in a nonsense assemblage of pipes and fittings.

3. Now comes the big part, the shading. The regular pencil is used to make a gradation of shading from the outside of the pipe and fittings inward. The white pencil is used to make a gradation of white shading that begins in the middle of the pipes and fittings and shades outwards. This makes for a perfect illusion of three-dimensional pipes. As an introduction to shading, this lesson is one of the best!

lesson 11 **See-Thru Pictures**

As an art teacher I sometimes see my role as that of a pied piper whose job it is to lead my kids off on paths that they otherwise would never have explored. This is another one of my pied piper lessons. It is fun, colorful, and very decorative!

you need:

- drawing paper
- pencil and crayons (or other drawing materials)

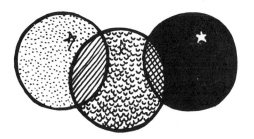

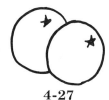

4-27

to present:

1. Explain to your class that under normal circumstances one object placed in front of another is drawn as shown in Figure 4-27.

Then go on to explain that today things are going to be different. In this lesson when one object is placed in front of another, both objects will be seen! (See Figure 4-28.)

4-28

2. For this lesson have your kids choose any kind of a picture idea that shows both a *container and that which is contained.* For example, Figure 4-29 shows a See-Thru fruit bowl with See-Thru fruit.*

4-29

3. The kicker comes when they have penciled in their pictures (in outline form) and are then told to change colors every time they cross a line!

lesson 12   **Pictures for Rubbing**

In Chapter 3 (*Magic Trace of Autumn*) and in lesson 6 of this chapter (*Martian Texture Hunt*) I have shown you two ways in which you can make *rubbings* using peeled

---

*Other examples might include a toy box with toys, a lunch box with lunch, a shopping bag with groceries, etc.

crayons. This lesson is the third in the series and this particular lesson has always been one of my favorites!

you need:

- plenty of drawing, construction, or tag paper (any size paper will do)
- pencil, scissors, paste or glue
- peeled crayons

to present:

1. Have your kids make and cut out a drawing of anything that suits their fancy. This picture is then pasted on top of another piece of paper. The important thing that they must remember is that *everything that is to register on the rubbing must be cut out and pasted.*

For example: to re-create the picture illustrated at the top of this page, the following steps were taken: (1) one uncut sheet became the background paper (see Figure 4-30A); (2) the house and the ground were cut out of another piece of paper and pasted to the first—the cloud was added in the same way (see Figure 4-30B); and (3) the windows and doors were cut out from scraps and pasted onto the house—the walk was added to the ground in the same way (see Figure 4-30C).

4-30A   4-30B   4-30C

lesson 13   **Trophy Time**

Not only is this mounted fish fun to make but it teaches a lot about fish!

you need:

- 9 x 12″ drawing paper

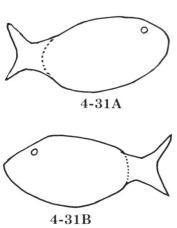

4-31A

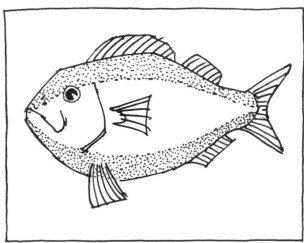

4-31B

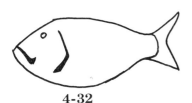

4-32

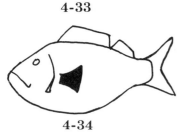

4-33

4-34

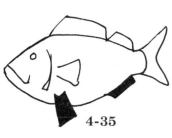

4-35

- 9 x 12″ dark background paper
- practice paper
- scissors, paste or glue
- pencil and crayons (or other decorating materials)

preliminary practice:

Since the more one knows about fish the better the likeness, it pays immediate dividends to spend a little time discussing basic fish anatomy before getting into the art end of this activity. Here's how I do it:

1. On a piece of practice paper I have my kids draw a freehand shape that looks something like the shapes in Figures 4-31A and 4-31B. Have them place an eye high on one end and a tail at the other.

2. Fish do not smile. Draw a grumpy mouth and add the curved gill-line. (See Figure 4-32.)

3. Most fish have the same fins. Some fish, however, have one back, or *dorsal*, fin while others have two—the *spiny* dorsal which is in front and the *soft* dorsal which is next to the tail. Draw one or two back, or dorsal, fins. (See Figure 4-33.)

4. The fin that corresponds to the arm is called the *pectoral* fin. It is located just behind the gills. Draw in this arm, or pectoral fin. (See Figure 4-34.)

5. The fin that corresponds to our leg is called the *pelvic* fin. This leg, or pelvic fin, extends down below the gill area. Draw it in. (See Figure 4-35.)

6. The last fin is the bottom, or *anal* fin. Draw in this fin and the fish is completed.

to present:

4-36

Once your kids have a basic concept of the anatomy of a fish, the rest is easy!

1. Have your kids draw a large *fat* fish on the 9 x 12″ drawing paper.

2. Now comes the tricky part. Each fish must have two lightly penciled curved lines that travel from the furthest point on the fish's head to the central end of the tail as shown here in Figure 4-36.

3. Once these gracefully drawn lines are sketched in, *score* these lines. Also score on the dotted lines indicated on Figure 4-37A.

4. When the scoring is complete, have your class color or decorate these fish in any way they desire. When they are done they are to be cut out.

5. When cut out and folded on the scored lines, the fish will take on a most realistic pose. Paste one *top* fin and one *bottom* fin to the 9 x 12″ background paper and your room will be filled with proud trophies!

The fish shown below is only a diagram to illustrate the way in which the scored lines are folded. A completed fish is as seen at the beginning of this lesson.

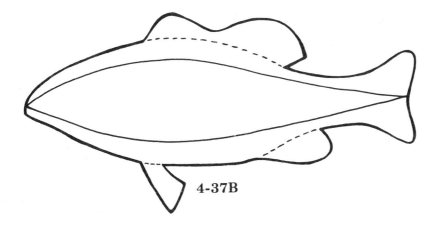

4-37B

lesson 14   **Freak-Outs**

When I first began to experiment with Freak-Outs they were simply a nameless diversion. It took a third grader in a school room in Edgartown, Massachusetts to christen them. This boy became so fascinated with the process that he looked up at me and blurted, "Holy Smokes, Mr. Baer, these're freak-outs!" So Freak-Outs they have remained.

you need:

- 6″ squares of white drawing or construction paper
- scissors and crayons

4-38

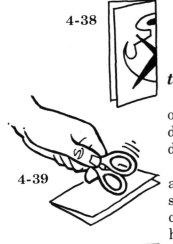

The Basic Freak-Out

to present:

1. Have your kids fold a 6″ square in half and with one or two crayons draw some kind of a design or decoration making sure that *some* part or parts of this drawing touches the center fold. (See Figure 4-38.)

4-39

2. The Freak-Out is then turned inside out and using a hard smooth metal scissor handle (or any other hard, smooth object) have your kids rub the back of the crayoned design with a firm, back and forth motion of the hand. (See Figure 4-39.)

3. When they open up the paper—*presto!*—the ghost of the first timid Freak-Out makes its appearance. (See Figure 4-40.)

4. To bring the Freak-Out to its full glory, simply touch up the faded image with fresh crayons.

4-40

Four-Square Freak-Outs

to present:

1. Fold the square in half and then in half again to make a small square. (See Figures 4-41A and 4-41B.) When ready for crayon, advise your kids to be certain that one or more parts of their design touches *both* of the folded edges as in Figure 4-41C.

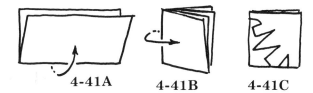

4-41A   4-41B   4-41C

2. This time when the design is folded inward, rubbed, and opened, the Freak-Out has only extended itself to *two* quadrants of the larger square. (See Figures 4-42A and 4-42B.) Freshen up these two quadrants with crayon and then refold to transfer this two quadrant design to the other half of the paper. (See Figure 4-42C.)

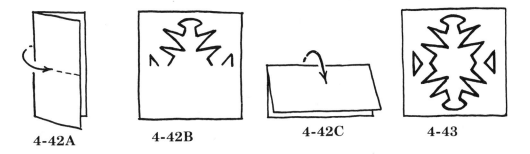

4-42A   4-42B   4-42C   4-43

3. Open up and touch up. The Four-Square Freak-Out is now complete! (See Figure 4-43.)

Suggestions: Try this same approach with a square folded on the diagonal!

lesson 15   **Junk Drawings**

I have never given this lesson without being impressed with the *quality* of the finished work!

you need:

- plenty of paper (duplicating or mimeograph paper will do fine)
- pens (fine-line markers are ideal but regular ball point pens will serve nearly as well)

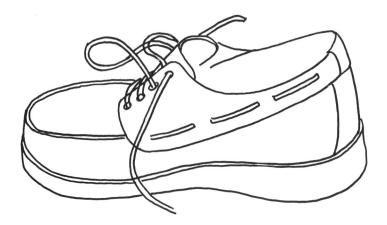

to present:

Drawing is knowledge. Some people who can "draw anything" are only demonstrating their remarkable memory for detail. Others of us who have poor to average memories must rely on firsthand information—we have to *see* what we want to draw.

For example, if you were to ask a child to draw, say, a stapler, the resulting drawing might not even be identifiable. But place a real stapler in front of this same child and the drawing will improve dramatically.

Give a child a pencil for drawing this stapler and the child will spend more time erasing than drawing. Give this same child a pen and explain that "since no one can erase, everyone's going to make mistakes," some really high quality work will emerge.

1. Arrange your children around tables or arrange their desks in clusters facing inward. In the center of each group place any kind of an object; a stapler, a pocketbook, an open watercolor box—whatever you can find—and ask them to draw it *as they see it* using line only (with no preliminary pencil drawing). That's it! Tell them that when they are done you will be back with more "junk" to draw.

2. *Your* job is to hustle around the room adding things to their tables for them to draw. If your room is relatively free of clutter, it might be a good idea to bring in a box of "junk" from home.

At one time or another I have used all kinds of things with great success but perhaps the most popular is somebody's shoe. Another popular item is a musical instrument. Even a cluster of keys makes a successful drawing!

Further Suggestions: If you are using standard-size (8½ x 11″) duplicating or mimeograph paper, the completed line drawing looks great when mounted on a 9 x 11½″ dark cuff against a 12 x 14″ white mount. (See pp. 256-259 for framing instructions and terminology.)

5

Holidays and Festivals

There are times when I feel that our holidays must have been created by Disneyland, for how else could a whole culture become looney enough to celebrate a fat man in a red suit, look forward to eggs left by a rabbit, or devote a whole holiday to a turkey?

Strangely enough, the more pious the occasion, the more outrageous the trappings—Santa Claus, Rudolf, the Easter Bunny! Look what happened to even a second stringer like St. Patrick's Day. It's been irreverently scrambled and dipped in green.

But don't knock these popular celebrations, for by reaching down to touch an unseen reality, they provide a very real and personal service. Santa, the Grinch, and a host of other fanciful characters may have little or nothing to do with the first Christmas, but they fill a real need that would otherwise remain unanswered. Children, I'm sure, instinctively know all of this.

After a certain age no one believes in Santa Claus or the Easter Bunny, nor do we necessarily grieve for our lost innocence. But Santa and all the rest of the mythology that populates the celebration of our holidays are what makes them fun—for in a very real sense, they celebrate life!

Columbus Day

Since neither the Phoenicians, Vikings, nor any of the other minority groups claiming discovery of America have a strong Washington lobby, Columbus Day continues to commemorate Columbus! Here are a few ideas to help your kids celebrate this memorable transatlantic crossing.

lesson 1 Columbus and the Briny Deep

you need:

- construction paper in the following sizes and colors:
    12 x 18″ light blue
    12 x 18″ assorted bright or light-colored (yellow excepted) "spooky sky" paper
    3 x 1⅛″ brown (approximate size)
    2″ square yellow
- scissors, and paste or glue
- crayons (or other decorating materials)

to present:

1. From one of the long edges of the light blue paper have your class cut off a strip an inch or so wide in such

a way as to suggest waves. The larger piece becomes the "water" paper and is pasted to the 12 x 18″ "sky" paper as in Figure 5-1. (Since we are trying to create an eerie mood, the more offbeat the color of the sky, the better.)

2. A few snips will turn the brown paper into a pretty fair primary-style Columbus boat. (See Figure 5-2.) Have your class paste this boat to the surface of the water, add a mast, decorate the yellow sail with a red cross and then paste the sail to the mast. (See lead illustration.)

3. Share with your class the sailors' fear of the unknown and have kids express this fear in the drawings of huge imaginary ocean dwellers. (All you have to do is *suggest*—your kids will do the rest!)

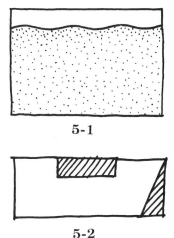

5-1

5-2

lesson 2   A Ship for Columbus

Here is an opportunity to combine a little Social Studies with your art lesson. Two, possibly three, of Columbus' ships were *caravels* and this gives your class an opportunity to learn a little bit about the nature of early ships. Although I do not pretend to be an expert on shipbuilding, the caravel that follows has more than a passing resemblance to the ship that must have carried Columbus to America.

you need:

- construction paper in the following colors and sizes:
  3 x 9″ brown
  12 x 18″ light blue
  6 x 9″ yellow
- scissors, and paste or glue
- crayons (or other decorating materials)

to present:

1. To make the ship, have your kids cut their 3 x 9″ brown paper as shown in the previous lesson, and paste this ship close to the bottom of the 12 x 18″ light blue paper. The three masts (the *mainmast*, the *foremast*, the *mizzenmast*) and the *bowsprit* are added with crayon. The mainmast should be the tallest of the three masts.

2. To make the sails, have your kids begin by folding the yellow sheet into four quadrants and then cutting on these folds. (See Figure 5-3.)

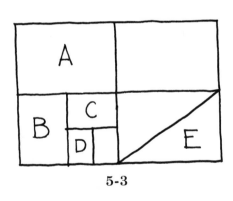

5-3

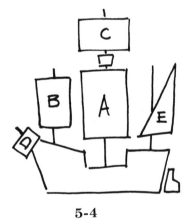

5-4

One of the four yellow pieces of "sail cloth" will become the *mainsail* (A). One of the other quadrants of sail cloth is cut in half widthwise to become the *foresail* (B). The remainder from the foresail is again cut in half widthwise to become the *topsail* (C). Half of the remainder from the topsail paper becomes the *spritsail* (D). Triangular piece (E) then becomes the lateen-rigged sail that brings up the rear.

For other Columbus Day activities see p. 78.

The final quadrant of sail cloth is not needed but can easily be used for making the pennants that fly from the top of the masts. (See illustration on p. 145.)

The sails can be pasted down flat as shown above or a more realistic portrayal of a ship under sail can be achieved by pasting only the forward edge of the sails; then, by lifting up the back edge of each sail so that it can "catch the wind," the picture becomes that much more exciting!

But of course you will also need a *crows-nest* and a *rudder* and a few additional accessories to make your ships seaworthy. Have your kids finish these pictures by illustrating one or more of the memorable scenes from the pages of this historic voyage.

Halloween

The Federal Government ignores it, the Church looks askance at it—if it wasn't for the kids it wouldn't exist at all. But don't underestimate Halloween—from a child's point of view this is the second most important "holiday" of the year.* If some way could be found to add wrapped presents to that pile of orange and black candy, Halloween would become—hands down—the greatest holiday of them all!

Even now it beats out birthdays.

lesson 3   ## Alley Cat

This is a popular lesson for many reasons, not the least of which lies in its decorative use of color.

you need:

- construction paper:
    12 x 18" gray
    6 x 4½" black (two each)

---

*Insofar as there is no suspension of business on Halloween, it is technically speaking not a "holiday" at all. (Kids, of course, could care less!)

assorted sizes of white, yellow, orange, and black

- 3½″ (watercup size) circle pattern
- pencil and black crayon
- scissors, and paste or glue

5-5A

to present:

1. To make a cat's head, have your kids trace the circle on one of the black pieces of paper. Add ears, cut on the heavy line, and assemble Circlecone style (see p. 38). Orange eyes and whiskers complete the head. (See Figures 5-5A and 5-5B.)

2. The other piece of black paper is for the cat's body. Although this body can be drawn in a number of different styles, some of your kids will welcome suggestions. One easy way to draw a simplified cat's body is to cut out a "door" out of the black paper and then use a piece of the cut-away scrap for the tail. (See Figure 5-6.)

3. Once the cats have been cut out, have your kids paste them to the gray background paper. (The cat's head, of course, must be pasted by the ears!)

4. From this point on, few suggestions will be necessary. Using assorted pieces of Halloween-colored paper and a black crayon, your kids will quickly get down to the business of adding bats, ghosts, haunted houses, and whatever else is needed to make a full-blooded Halloween picture. (See lead illustration.)

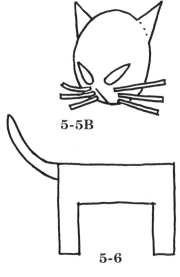

5-5B

5-6

Further Suggestions: In order to attend to everyone's paper needs while at the same time minimizing waste, I sometimes find it convenient to open a "store." Tearing up the colored papers into convenient-sized pieces, I have the kids come forward to take whatever paper they need to get started. The children are invited to return to the "store" as often as the need arises (while I spend my time furiously tearing up paper into convenient sizes to replace the quickly diminishing piles).

Since kids love make believe, you will find this store game to be a good way of organizing all kinds of activities that call for a wide spectrum of papers.

lesson 4 Giant Masks

Mask-making is always a popular activity. Based upon the Sailboat Cone (see *Your Basic Bag Of Tricks*, p. 52), these oversized masks are guaranteed to be the hit of the day!

you need:

- construction paper:
    one 18 x 24″ or two 12 x 18″
        light colors
    6 x 18″ dark colors
    6 x 4½″ assorted colors
- scissors, and paste or glue
- crayons (or other decorating
    materials)

to present:

1. The first prerequisite is one *large* piece of paper. If the 18 x 24″ size is not available, then have your kids make an approximate equivalent by pasting together two 12 x 18″ pieces. Following the instructions on page 52, turn this sheet into a basic Sailboat Cone.

In order to gain some insight into how this cone will eventually evolve into a Giant Mask, here is a preview of what's to come:

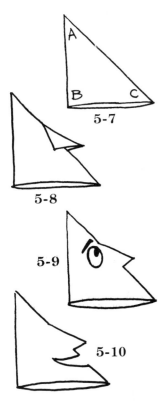

5-7

5-8

5-9

5-10

The apex of the cone (A) will become the top of the head. The square corner (B), the back of the neck. The remaining corner (C) will become the chin. (See Figure 5-7.) Because of the great size of this mask, the cut-away mouth will serve a double purpose, for all seeing will have to be done through this opening. The apparent eyes of the mask are purely decorative!

2. Now back to specific recommendations and suggestions.

The Nose. Using one of the 6 x 4½″ papers, have your kids make a Sailboat Fold Nose as shown on p. 37. Paste so that the lateral edges of the nose overlap both sides of the face. (See Figure 5-8.)

The Eyes. The eyes can be as simple as big white paper circles decorated with black pupils, and eyebrows can also be added. (See Figure 5-9.)

The Mouth. Although the cutout mouth can be left toothless, a few added, scattered white teeth are recommended—other details such as a tongue, a cigar, etc., are always worth at least passing consideration! (See Figure 5-10.)

The Ears. Ears can be made any size but a couple of 6 x 4½″ papers will do nicely. One way to make ears, complete with pasting tabs, is shown in Figures 5-11A, 5-11B and 5-11C:

Head and Hair. The top of the head can be finished in many ways. Here are a few suggestions (see Figures 5-12A and 5-12B):

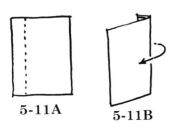

5-11A

5-11B

5-11C

Pointed Head	Flat Head
Just leave the head the way it is and add hair.	Simply cut off the pointed apex and add hair. (The dark 6 x 18″ strips work well here.)

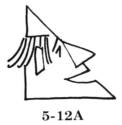

5-12A

5-12B

Hats. Hats are optional, but since some of the more ambitious members of your class may seek your advice as to hat-making ideas, here is a quick and easy way to make a pointed witch's style hat:

The crown of the hat is a cone made from a sheet of 9 x 12″ black construction paper (see the *Perfect Sailboat Cone* pp. 52-53).

To make the brim of the hat, cut out a black construction paper circle approximately 12″ in diameter. In the middle of this circle cut a number of radial lines as shown in Figure 5-13.

5-13

To prepare the mask for the hat, stuff a ball of paper into the apex of the mask to give the top of the head a firm conical shape.

The way in which the brim and the crown are assembled and pasted are indicated in Figures 5-14A, 5-14B and 5-14C. The brim goes on first, followed immediately by the crown. Note that the crown pastes over the radial flaps of the brim.

| 5-14A | 5-14B | 5-14C |

lesson 5 **The Haunted House**

The Sixteen-Part Box Fold (see *Your Basic Bag of Tricks*, p. 32) can be used in many different ways. And for a haunted house it can't be beat!

you need:

- construction paper:
    - 12 x 18″ black
    - 6 x 4½″ black
    - 6 x 4½″ white
- small scraps of orange
- pencils, scissors, and paste or glue

to present:

1. Follow the instructions for the Sixteen-Part Box but stop before the actual pasting. (See Figure 5-15.)

2. Using Figure 5-16 as a general guide, have your kids decorate the interior of their "ghost house." They will need little encouragement to use their small pieces of black and white paper to add windows, doors (trap doors?), etc. (Those areas indicated by shading will be lost in the foldup.)

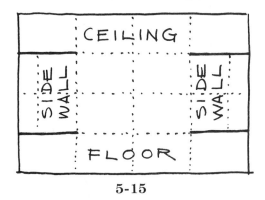

5-15

5-16

Other *Halloween* ideas can be found on pp. 82 and 219.

3. Once this project is well underway, pass out small scraps of orange paper. Your kids will find a use for them!

Once the rooms are fairly well organized they can be assembled and pasted. (A stapler, if you have one, would be welcome here.) Once assembled, encourage your class to add furniture, stand-up figures, or whatever else is needed to complete the room.

Further Suggestions: If you are not totally at home in cut paper work, I would suggest that you review the *Ins and Outs of Cut Paper*, p. 54.

For stand-up ghosts, follow the instructions for the Sailboat Ghost (p. 53), but substitute 6 x 4½″ white paper for the 12 x 18″.

For an eye-stopping bulletin board, assemble the rooms into houses, and add roofs, chimneys, etc.

Thanksgiving

The history books still have difficulty supporting that old chestnut about the cosmopolitan Pilgrims and the wild but childlike Indians, for, contrary to what a lot of us were led to believe, the New World of 1620 wasn't all that new!

Since Europeans had been poking around the New England shores for a hundred years prior to the landing of the Mayflower, it should come as no surprise to learn that many of the Indians could already speak passable English. Samoset, as you might remember, welcomed the Pilgrims in their own tongue, and since Squanto had twice been to Europe, it follows that he too was multilingual.*

Granted that the Pilgrims did not eat at Howard Johnson's or stay at a Holiday Inn, but somehow, a second examination of the Plymouth Colony adds more than a thoughtful query to the traditional spirit of this celebration.

The Spirit of Giving Thanks, however, is something we all understand and no amount of historical fact-

---

*Since he had most recently been on an extended visit to Spain, it is reasonable to suppose that Squanto could have just as easily greeted them in Spanish!

grubbing can overshadow the knowledge that children love this time of the year—and *that* recommendation is certainly good enough for me!

lesson 6   **The Hand-Gobbler**

Although there is nothing particularly original about using a hand to draw a bird, this Hand-Gobbler has a few more frills than your normal run-of-the-mill schoolroom turkey. Furthermore, regardless of the age level with which you work, this turkey can be easily adapted to meet your needs!

you need:

- paper and pencil
- crayons (or other decorating materials)

to present:

1. Have your children trace one of their hands. (See Figure 5-17A.) Add a triangle for a wing and complete the breast line. Add legs and feet. (See Figure 5-17B.)

2. Add eye, beak, and any other details desired. This

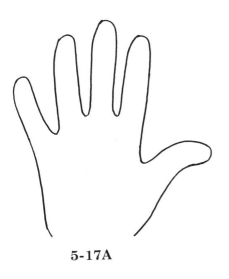

5-17A

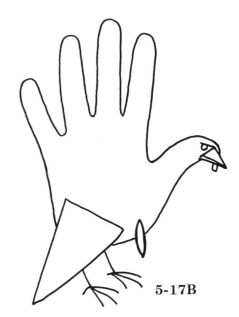

5-17B

turkey can be as simple or as complicated as the artists that draw them. (It may not be perfect, but it's easier than trying to draw a hand by tracing a turkey!)

lesson 7   **Thanksgiving A-Cone Turkey**

Although I don't use the A-Cone often, it supplies a dramatic answer to certain kinds of three-dimensional problems. Your class will love this one!

you need:

- construction paper:
    6 x 9″ gray or brown
    6 x 1″ strip of red
- 12 x 18″ drawing paper
- scissors, and paste or glue
- crayons (or other decorating materials)

to present:

1. Explain to your class that they must think up a picture idea in which a large turkey will play a key roll.*

---

*Suggestions: "Chasing a Turkey," "Looking for a Turkey," etc.

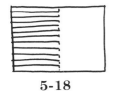

5-18

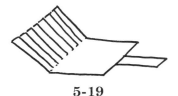

5-19

5-20

Explain also that they must begin this picture immediately but that the turkeys will arrive later. Once this part of the lesson is underway on the 12 x 18" drawing paper, pass out the rest of the paper supplies.

2. Steps 2—4 deal with the making of the turkey. Have your kids fold the 6 x 9" "turkey" paper in half widthwise and make a series of cuts to the fold as illustrated in Figure 5-18.

3. With the paper placed down on their desks and the "tail feathers" in an *up* position, have your kids put a little paste on the end of the red strip and paste this strip under the center of the uncut end. (See Figure 5-19.)

4. When the paste has had time to set, staple the breast of the turkey into an open A-Cone position. Fold the end of the red strip so that it looks like a head and then point the beak. Add eyes. (See Figure 5-20.)

5. Now comes the time when the turkey is to be pasted to the drawing paper!

When pasting the turkey feathers to the paper, be sure that the part of the feathers that is next to the body receives a careful pasting to the picture, for this will be the part of the pasting job that will receive the greatest stress. Once the turkey is pasted into position, have your kids add the turkey legs, and with that their picture is complete!

lesson 8   **Thanksgiving Diorama**

If you think of dioramas in terms of shoe boxes, you're in for a pleasant surprise. This diorama is not assembled until *after* the background is finished!

you need:

- 12 x 18" and 4½" white or manila drawing paper
- scissors, and paste or glue
- crayons (or other decorating materials)

Other *Thanksgiving* ideas can be found on pp. 85, 86, and 226.

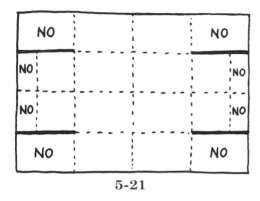

5-21

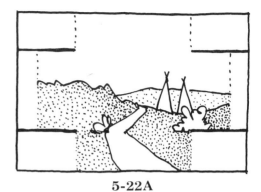

5-22A

to present:

1. Construct a box using the Sixteen-Part Box Fold (see *Your Basic Bag of Tricks*, p. 32), but have your class stop before the actual pasting. Instead, as shown in Figure 5-21, have your kids write the word "no" in the areas indicated.

2. I often use "no" areas to simplify instructions. In this lesson the "no's" are used to efficiently eliminate the non-pictorial parts of this diorama.

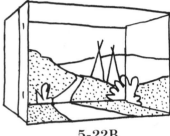

5-22B

Figures 5-22A and 5-22B below show how this works. The first picture illustrates those parts of the diorama that are to be drawn and colored; the second, how this same odd-shaped picture appears when the box is assembled and pasted for permanency.

3. The diorama is complete when the artist adds a few appropriate stand-up props to the picture. The easiest way to make stand-ups is simply to allow for a pasting tab as shown in Figures 5-23A and 5-23B. (Other stand-up ideas can be found on p. 19.)

Stand-up suggestions might include tents, cabins, bushes, turkeys, Indians, Pilgrims, etc.

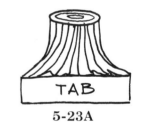

TAB

5-23A

5-23B

Christmas

In our democratic concern for the separation of church and state, it is conceivable that our public school system may someday be forced to cancel observances of all but the most nationalistic of holidays.* If this becomes the case, Christmas and Easter will be the first to go.

But there are those who will argue that these holidays are already gone—for the Grinch and the Easter Bunny have about as much to do with religion as a McDonald's Shamrock Shake has to to with the life of Saint Patrick!

lesson 9   **Christmas Kings (and Queens)**

In writing a book entitled *Paste, Pencils, Scissors and Crayons*, I am naturally a little reluctant to include activities in which success depends upon a *stapler*! On the other hand I am not that much of a purist that I am going to throw away a really good lesson just because it can't be hammered into shape to fit an abbreviated title. *Christmas Kings* is that kind of lesson. Your kids will love it!

you need:

- construction paper:
    6 x 24″ (or one 6 x 18″ and one 6 x 9″) crown-colored
    12 x 18″ assorted hair-colored
    odd scraps jewel-colored
- scissors, and paste or glue
- stapler

to present:

1. A long strip of paper is needed to make a crown. If you do not have 6 x 24″ paper, paste together the 6 x 18″ and the 6 x 9″. Fold this long paper lengthwise and then fold both long edges back to touch the centerline as shown in Figures 5-24A and 5-24B. The end result resembles an extended M or a W, as in Figure 5-24C.

2. Unfold the last two folds and have your class make a series of cuts as shown in Figure 5-25. Each cut *must* go all the way to the longitudinal creases.

---

*Take a look at the holidays on a Soviet calendar. The Russian child celebrates Soviet Army Day (Feb. 23rd), International Women's Day (March 8th), International Holiday of Working People's Solidarity (May 1st & 2nd), Victory Day of Our People in the Great Patriotic War (May 9th), and the anniversary of the October Revolution (Nov. 7 & 8th). Wow!

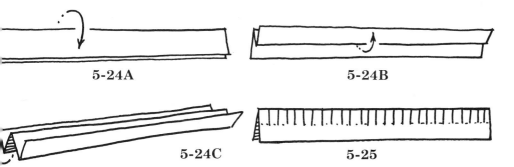

5-24A 5-24B

5-24C 5-25

3. The hair is prepared by making long parallel cuts widthwise on the 12 x 18″ "hair" piece and pasting it to the inside of the crown as in Figure 5-26. (A staple to anchor both ends of this hair paper to the crown would be a good idea.)

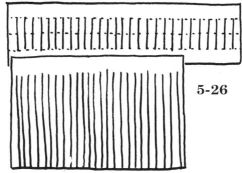

5-26

4. Here is where you as a teacher really begin to earn your pay. Each of these crowns must be individually fitted (wrapped snugly to each head) and stapled top and bottom. The fitting and stapling is easy but since most of your class will be finishing about the same time, all will be clambering to have theirs done first!

5. In order to individualize each crown (as well as to allow you time to organize your fitting line), pass out the small scraps of colored paper and have your kids begin to enrich their crowns with jewels.

6. Once the crown has been fitted and stapled, some of the children will object to having too much hair in the face area. This complaint can be easily remedied with a few royal snips of the scissors.

And Finally: For the best of all possible endings, have your kids *curl* their hair (see *Three Ways of Curling Paper*, p. 44).

lesson 10   **Holiday Candle**

In my personal bag of tricks there are certain lessons that are timeless, and this is one of them!

you need:

- construction paper:
    two strips 3 x 18″ red or green
    9 x 12″ black
    3″ square (any color)
    decorating scraps
- stapler, and paste or glue

to present:

1. Begin by having your class paste the two long strips together to make one *very* long strip. While that is drying, turn to the 9 x 12″ black paper.

2. Fold the black paper in half widthwise and have your kids cut a small V shaped notch in the center of the fold.(See Figure 5-27A.) Once the notch has been cut, open this paper and fold it into quarters as shown in Figures 5-27B and 5-27C.

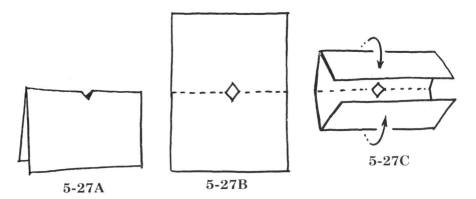

5-27A   5-27B   5-27C

3. Returning now to the long strip of paper prepared in step 1, have your kids roll it into a tube with an inside diameter about the size of one of their fingers. (See

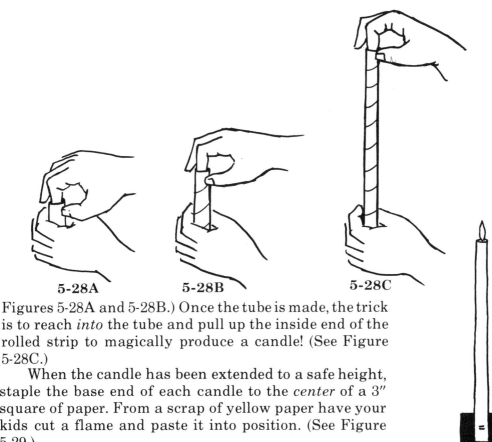

5-28A   5-28B   5-28C

5-29

Figures 5-28A and 5-28B.) Once the tube is made, the trick is to reach *into* the tube and pull up the inside end of the rolled strip to magically produce a candle! (See Figure 5-28C.)

When the candle has been extended to a safe height, staple the base end of each candle to the *center* of a 3″ square of paper. From a scrap of yellow paper have your kids cut a flame and paste it into position. (See Figure 5-29.)

Detailed Candle Instructions. If pulled out too far, the candle will collapse, if not rolled tightly enough the candle will be fat and unsightly, but when done properly it is a childhood masterpiece. To *assure* a roomful of successful candles I would recommend that the teacher become familiar with the ways of this candle *before* the lesson begins.

The first trick to learn is that a loosely wound candle tube can be tightened by placing a finger inside the tube and twisting in a motion similar to that of winding a watch. (One way tightens, the other, loosens.) Once the tube has been extended into a candle it can be tightened again using a similar twisting motion.

4. Once the candles are secure, the rest is easy. The candles are put through the center hole in the 9 x 12″ black paper and this black paper is then folded up into a triangular base. (See Figure 5-30 and lead illustration.)

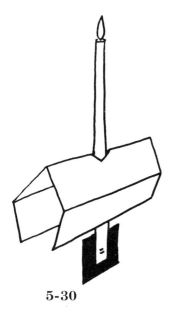

5-30

The 3″ square need not be pasted for it flattens out against the bottom of the triangular base to become an adjustable "foot." (See Figure 5-30.)

5. When complete, make odds and ends of colored paper available so that the kids can add their personal touches of seasonal decoration.

lesson 11   Holiday Stars

How do you make a star? The first answer should be to turn to p. 46. The second answer is a little bit more complicated. I do not recommend trying to teach this lesson to large classes of small children. Instead, keep this lesson in readiness for those special occasions that demand the *perfect* star.

Drawn Stars

you need:

- paper
- pencil
- compass
- scissors

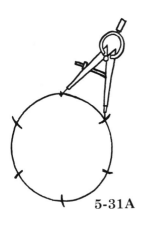

5-31A

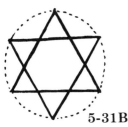

5-31B

to make:

The Six-Point Star. Draw a circle, and then with the same radius "walk" the compass around the circle. (See Figure 5-31A.) If your compass is accurate you will have divided the circle into six equal parts. Connect the points as shown in Figure 5-31B and the result is a six-point star.

The Five-Point Star. Begin by drawing a circle but this time open the compass just a little larger so that it reaches around the circumference exactly five times. (See Figure 5-32A.) This is a trial and error job but it is not as difficult as it sounds. Connect the points as shown in Figure 5-32B to make a perfect five-point star.

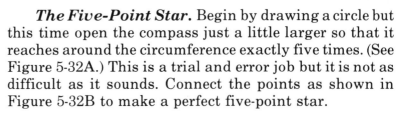

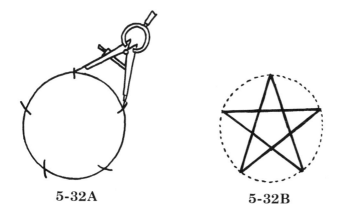

5-32A   5-32B

Folded Paper Stars

Although these folded paper stars depend upon a little trial and error guesswork, both are well worth the time and effort that it takes to master them!

you need:
- square pieces of paper
- scissors

to make:

The Six-Point Star. Fold the paper in half diagonally. To find the center, fold lightly in half lengthwise and unfold. Using this found center as the pivot point, fold the lefthand side over so that the neighboring angles formed by the "A" and "B" section at the bottom center of the paper are equal. Segment B is then folded over to rest on top of segment A. Cut on a bias (as indicated by the dotted line) and open up. The result is a six-point star!

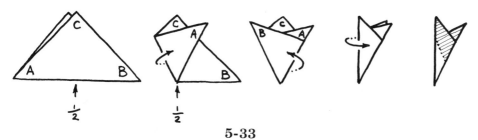

5-33

The Five-Point Star. Begin as in the previous paragraph but this time the angle formed at the bottom of the A section must be *twice* that of the corresponding B section. Fold B back over A and fold the remainder of A over B. Cut as before and open up to reveal a five-point star!

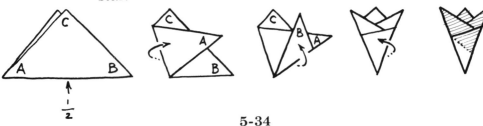

5-34

lesson 12   **A Self-Sealing Greeting Card**

Over half of all personal mail in this country is sent in the form of a greeting card. No wonder that card-making is such a popular classroom activity!

you need:

- construction paper:
    12 x 18″ light-colored
    odds and ends of assorted scraps
- pencils, scissors, paste or glue
- crayons (or other decorating materials)

to present:

1. Fold the large paper in half widthwise. Open up and fold the ends into the center. Open up and fold about 2″ of the long sides in towards the center. (See Figure 5-35.)

2. Cut off the shaded areas and the basic self-sealing envelope is complete. (See Figure 5-36.)

3. Decorate the inside of the card with an appropriate design and message. (See Figure 5-37.)

4. Fold up the card and tuck in the flaps as in Figure 5-38A. Where the flaps tuck in write the instructions "open here" as in Figure 5-38B.

5. And that's it—address the other side, affix postage, and mail it!

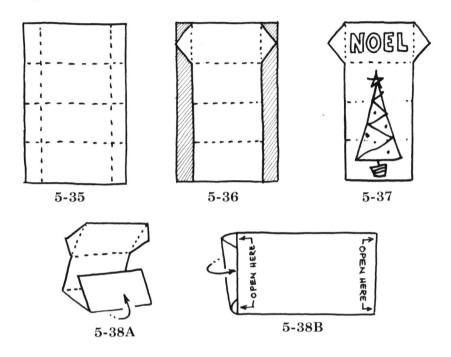

5-35   5-36   5-37

5-38A   5-38B

lesson 13   The Christmas Snake

Although I have arrived too late on the scene to invent Rudolf, the Great Pumpkin, the Grinch, or Frosty the Snowman, I am not beyond trying my hand at creating a few new folk heroes of my own. To date my most memorable success has been the Christmas Snake. Already there are hundreds of children in my neighborhood who believe in the Christmas Snake just as sincerely as you and I believe in Donner and Blitzen.

And like all good mythological creatures, the Christmas Snake fills a needed role. As you are well aware, right before Christmas the most mysterious part of the child's home is that closet in which the parents have stored the bulk of their presents. It is to add to this mystery that I have invented the story of the faithful Christmas Snake, the zealous guardian of the gifts. It is *he* who lies in wait among the secret clutter of a high shelf to frighten away any intruders who would be foolish enough to want to peek into the forbidden closets of Christmas.

If you need an opener for this activity, you might begin by reminding your class of the old poem that begins:

"T'was the night before Christmas
And all through the house
Something came slithering
And ate up the mouse ..."

If their memories need further jogging, continue with:

"The stockings were hung
By the chimney with care,
In hopes that the Christmas Snake
Soon would be there!"

you need:

- construction paper:
    12 x 18″ green
    3 x 4½″ red
    ¾ x 7″ white
    scraps of assorted colors

For other *Christmas*-related ideas see pp. 87, 91, and 204.

  • 18″ (or longer) ruler or tag strip
  • scissors, and paste or glue
  • pencil

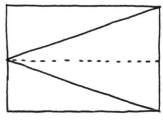

5-39

to present:

1. Have your class fold their 12 x 18″ green paper in half lengthwise, then unfold it. Lines are then drawn from one end of this fold to each of the far corners. (See Figure 5-39.) Cut on these drawn lines (and save the cut-away shaded parts for later).

2. The long edges of this large triangular shape are then folded into the middle fold as shown in Figure 5-40.

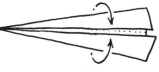

5-40

3. The paper is unfolded again to be refolded on the center fold. Keeping the center fold at the top, as shown in Figure 5-41A, have your kids draw a series of diagonal lines down the back of the "snake" and then cut on these lines. Be sure that each cut touches the creased lines. For a better mouth, remove the shaded section.

5-41A

Fold up and paste. Add eyes from scraps of colored paper, and trim the lower lip. (See Figure 5-41B.)

5. Legs, wings, etc., are an optional use of the green scraps that were saved from step 1.

5-41B

6. To make the Santa hat, fold the red paper according to the instructions for the Sailboat Cone, p. 52. The ¾ x 7″ white strip is for the fringe. Use a scrap of white for the pom-pom. A Santa Claus beard is optional!

5-41C

New Year's

Successful holiday activities feed upon anticipation. Since getting there is half the fun, the trouble with New Year's is that it is over by the time the kids return from Christmas Recess. This, of course, does not mean that you can't have a successful New Year's lesson, but it does mean trying to heat up some leftover interest in a holiday that is already yesterday's news!

Although I have dozens of good pre-Christmas lessons, my post-New Year's are limited to a handful of tried-and-trues. Here are two of my best. The first generates interest by focusing on the *baby* part of New Year's and the second is offbeat enough to capture anyone's interest!

lesson 14 **New Year's Baby**

Since babies are always popular, New Year's makes as good a time as any to learn how to draw children!

you need:

- construction paper:
    6 x 4½" flesh-colored
    6 x 9" flesh-colored
    6x 4½" diaper white
- 9 x 12" manila drawing paper
- 3½" (watercup size) circle patterns
- scissors, and paste or glue
- crayons or other decorating materials)

to present:

1. Have your kids trace the circle patterns on the small flesh-colored paper. Children, you explain, look like children because they are shaped like children. To draw a convincing child's head, have your kids draw the eyes, nose, mouth, and ears, *low* on the circle. Add hair. After the drawings are complete, have your kids cut them out. (See Figure 5-42.)

2. One way to make the body is to use the 6 x 9″ flesh-colored paper to make a Full-Paper Star (see p. 48) as in Figure 5-43A. Cut out the star, add the head, and trim away the excess paper under the "arms." (See Figure 5-43B.) The body is then folded as indicated by the dotted lines. To locate the three points of the fitted diapers, lay the center of the body onto the white paper and mark off the limits of the diaper before cutting. (See Figure 5-43C.)

5-43A

5-43B

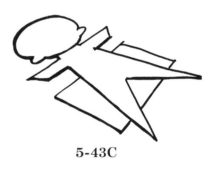

5-43C

3. The braided rug is easy to make.* Have your kids cut out an oval shape from the 9 x 12″ manila and begin their spiral from the middle of the paper. When colored, have your kids change crayons often to simulate a braided rug effect. (See Figure 5-44.)

5-44

---

*Strangely enough, many young children have difficulty with the whole concept of cutting a round corner. Instead of Figure 5-45A, they have Figure 5-45B:

5-45A

5-45B

lesson 15   **A Chinese
New Year's Fish**

Not all cultures celebrate New Year's as we do.
Whereas we may think of New Year's in terms of confetti
and babies, for the Chinese it's firecrackers and kites. In
this lesson we are going to make a festive oriental-style
fish, an open-mouthed carp-like creation that can be used
either to float in the wind (which makes it, technically,
not a kite but a wind sock) or hung from the ceiling like a
mobile. Either way it makes for a happy lesson!

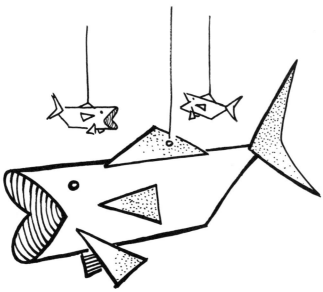

you need:

- 12 x 18″ construction paper in assorted colors
- scissors, and paste or glue

to present:

1. Fold the paper lengthwise, slightly off center as
shown in Figure 5-46A. Fold up and paste tab A. (See
Figure 5-46B.

2. Make two Sailboat Folds (see p. 37) at the same end
and cut through this double thickness of paper to remove
shaded area B. (See Figure 5-47.) Save the two B pieces for
later.

3. Sailboat Fold the other end—once only—and cut

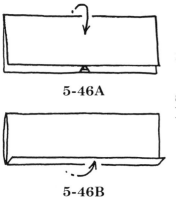

5-46A

5-46B

out the *top* (single thickness) triangle C and save this piece for later. (See Figure 5-48A.) Bottom triangle C is then folded up and pasted to seal this end of the fish. (See Figure 5-48B.)

4. Each child will then trade all three of the saved triangles for all three of another color. (In order to arrive at a trade in which all children end up with another color, it is sometimes necessary to have some of the children trade once again.)

5. Have your kids add an eye to their fish as shown. The small B triangles (saved from step 2) are then cut in half to make the pectoral and pelvic fins as shown in Figure 5-49.

6. Cut the large C triangle (saved from step 3) on the dotted line to make the tail and the dorsal fin. (See Figures 5-50A and 5-50B.)

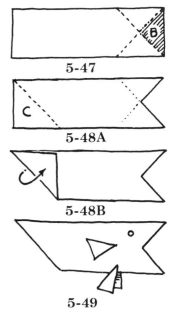

5-47

5-48A

5-48B

5-49

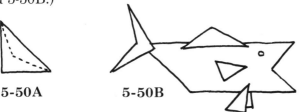

5-50A 5-50B

To Use Your Fish for Room Decorations. To fill out the fish, stuff the body with scrap paper. To hang, punch a hole in the dorsal fin and hang from a string (see lead illustration).

To Use Your Fish as Wind Socks. Use tissue paper instead of construction paper, and install a lightweight wire around the inside of the mouth to keep it open. Fasten a thread to the upper lip and let the fish float in the wind. (See Figure 5-51.)

5-51

Birthdays

Birthdays are always fun but, from a child's point of view, presidential birthdays are on the low end of the popularity scale. With no presents and no feast involved, they have never even had a competitor's chance. Furthermore, our two best-known presidential birthdays, Washington's and Lincoln's, are tucked in the shadow of St. Valentine's Day. Just think, if either of these gentlemen had only been born in a month with less competition—who knows, they might have become famous!

lesson 16   **Happy Birthday!**

Since February seems to be a big birthday month, I sometimes just have the kids make a paper cake.

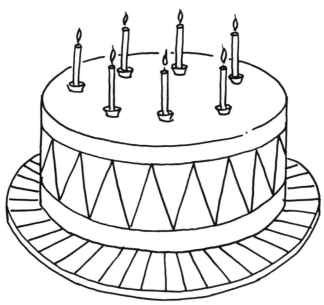

you need:

- white paper in the following sizes:
    9 x 12″ for cake 1
    12 x 18″ for cake 2
- pencil and crayons (or other decorating materials)

to present:

The Simple Cake

1. To make this birthday cake, your kids are going to have to learn how to draw a cylinder. It's easy: (1) first you draw a pickle (see Figure 5-52A), (2) then draw a line down from each end of the pickle (see Figure 5-52B), and (3) add a smiling line (see Figure 5-52C).*

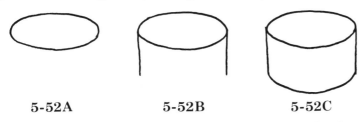

<table>
<tr><td>5-52A</td><td>5-52B</td><td>5-52C</td></tr>
</table>

5-53A

2. To add a plate to this cylinder-cake, simply place a dot on each side of the cake (see Figure 5-53A), and connect these two dots with a curved line as shown in Figure 5-53B.

3. To add candles (which are in themselves little cylinders), have your kids lightly pencil a "pickle" on the top central surface of their cakes. (See Figure 5-54A.) Each candle must be drawn so that the base touches this oval construction line as in Figure 5-54B. (Be sure to remind your kids to make each candle in an *upright* position.)

5-53B

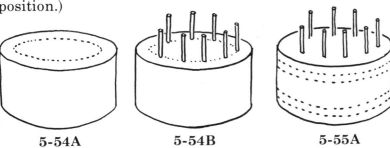

<table>
<tr><td>5-54A</td><td>5-54B</td><td>5-55A</td><td>5-55B</td></tr>
</table>

Further Suggestions: The cake, as well as the plate, can be decorated in a number of ways, but you should advise your class against the use of horizontal lines. Note how many curved "smiling" lines are used to decorate the cake shown in Figures 5-55A and 5-55B.

---

*I call it a *smiling line* because it resembles a smile. (What would you call it?)

The Supercake

1. To make a tier cake is simply a matter of learning how to add one cake on top of another, but for some reason or other many kids have trouble with this concept, so take your time with the instructions and don't take too much for granted. Here is how it's done (see Figures 5-56A, 5-56B, 5-56C and 5-56D):

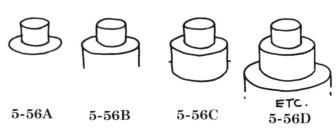

5-56A   5-56B   5-56C   ETC. 5-56D

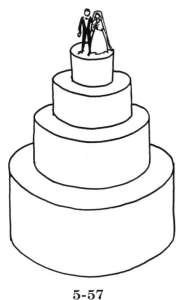

5-57

Further Suggestions: The Supercake is an all-around lesson that can be used for nearly any occasion; with hearts it's a Valentine cake, with Shamrocks it's a Leprechaun's delight. Put a bride and groom at the top and you have a wedding cake, or use a basketball player and you have a victory cake! (See Figure 5-57.)

lesson 17   A Hat for Abe

You'll find many off-season uses for this "Abraham Lincoln" hat. It can be used for everything from Halloween costumes to classroom melodramas. (It's also good for producing rabbits!)

you need:

- black construction paper in the following sizes:
  - 9 x 24″ or 9 x 18″ + 9 x 9″
  - 3 x 24″ or 3 x 18″ + 3 x 9″
  - 12″ square
- 12″ (shy) circle pattern
- 3½″ (watercup size) circle pattern
- pencil, scissors, paste or glue
- stapler

to present:

1. As suggested in the needs list, an Abraham Lincoln hat needs a long piece of black paper. If the 24″ paper is not available, have your class paste together the 9 x 18″ to the 9 x 9″ and the 3 x 18″ to the 3 x 9″.

2. The circle patterns are used to make concentric circles on the 12″ black square. Have your kids cut out the large circle and cut away the inside circle so that a large donut shape remains. Radius segment lines are then drawn to within approximately 2″ of the outside edge as shown here. Cut on these lines. (See Figure 5-58.)

3. The larger piece of black paper is individually fitted to the wearer's head and stapled to size. Now comes the hard part—slipping the hat brim over the crown until the brim is as shown in Figure 5-59. The upright tabs can be either stapled or pasted (stapler preferred). The throat of a large stapler will easily slip over the brim to do the job.

4. The remaining long strip is the hatband. Simply paste or staple to fit! (See Figure 5-60.)

Further Suggestions: For a fun-style top hat, use a colored band and add a bow (see Figure 5-61), or you might even want to try a light-colored hat with a dark hat band! (See Figure 5-62.)

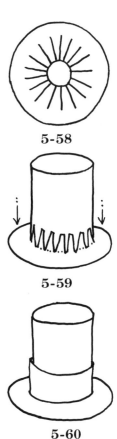

5-58

5-59

5-60

5-61   5-62

lesson 18   **1776 (George Washington) Hats**

Although the call for these hats is not overwhelming, when you need a 1776 hat it is always nice to know how to make one!

you need:

- blue construction paper in the following sizes:
   three pieces of 4½ x 12″
   3 x 24″ or 3 x 18″ plus 3 x 9″
- stapler, scissors, and pencils

to present:

1. As in the previous lesson, if the 24″ paper is not available, paste together a 3 x 18″ and a 3 x 9″ to make one long sheet. This is the hat band and must be individually fitted and stapled. (See Figure 5-63.)

2. The three remaining pieces are used to make the three sides of the hat. Cut away the shaded portion of all three pieces as indicated in Figure 5-64.

3. Staple the corner of the three side pieces as shown in Figure 5-65A. Position the hat band, and center-staple to all three sides. (See Figure 5-65B.) Your hat is now ready for the next parade!

5-63

5-64

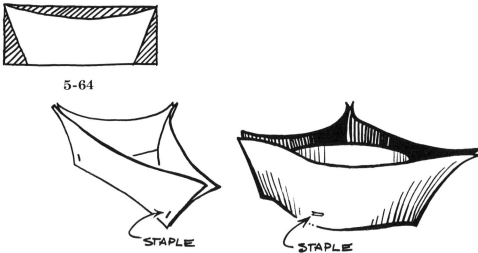

5-65A   5-65B

Valentine's Day

Although many children are too shy to admit it, Valentine's Day is just as important a day on their calendar as it is on mine! Here are two good lessons to help you celebrate this occasion.

lesson 19   **A Five Dollar Valentine⚛**

This valentine has style, dignity, and an element of surprise that makes it one of my all-time favorites. Your kids will love it!

you need:

- construction paper:
    - 9 x 12″ white
    - 9 x 12″ red
    - 3 x 9″ red (two each)
    - 6 x 4½″ red

- scissors, and paste or glue

to present:

1. Both 9 x 12″ papers are to be folded in half widthwise. The white paper, however, is taken one step further. While the white paper is folded, fold each of the sides up to touch the center fold as shown in Figure 5-66. (If folded correctly it will resemble either an M or a W.)

2. The two outside surfaces of the folded white paper are then pasted to the red paper as shown in Figure 5-67.

3. The 3 x 9″ pieces are then folded in half widthwise, and then in half again. Using the "snowflake" approach (see p. 98), have your kids cut pieces from all four edges of these folded parcels. (If you have lightweight red paper, by all means use it.) These red lacy pieces are used to decorate the side panels. (See Figure 5-68A.)

4. Have your kids fold the 4½ x 6″ red piece to make a heart (see p.103). This heart can then be cut out and pasted to straddle the inner white centerfold. (See Figure 5-68B.)

Alternate Method: A more elaborate card (a *ten* dollar valentine?) can be made by cutting out a heart in

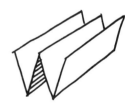

5-66

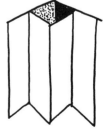

5-67

---

*To put a price tag on a classroom valentine is of course pure nonsense but it is the sort of nonsense that children love!

5-68A

5-68B

5-68C

the center of the white paper before it is pasted down (see step 1). If this method is used, substitute a white heart for step 3 and paste this heart in the recessed "cave." (See Figure 5-68C.)

lesson 20   Hearts A'Flutter

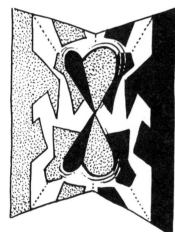

Although this is a little bit more complicated than the previous valentine, you'll find the results well worth the trouble!

you need:

- construction paper:
    - 9 × 12″ red
    - 9″ square red
    - 9″ square white
- pencil, scissors, and paste or glue

to present:

1. The 9 x 12″ red paper is to be folded in half width-wise and then set aside for use later in the lesson.

2. Have your kids fold the 9″ red paper horizontally, vertically, and in both directions diagonally. (See Figure 5-69.) For best results have them reverse each fold so as to destroy its "memory."

3. Then have this paper folded into a square packet as shown in Figure 5-70A and place the packet before them with the four-cornered end positioned to the upper left. The heart is then drawn as shown and the shaded area cut away. Note that the side of the heart is on the fold (as represented by the dotted line) and is *not* cut. When

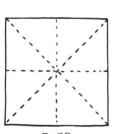

5-69

Other Valentine lessons can be found on pp. 103 and 104.

opened, the result should look like Figure 5-70B.

4. The *triangular* areas of this paper are then pasted to the larger red paper (see step 1) so that the center folds are aligned. (See Figure 5-71.) Be sure that your kids understand that the hearts are *not* to be pasted!

5. The white paper is twice folded on the diagonal (see Figure 5-72A), and then cut "snowflake" style (see p. 98). When done, have the kids open their "snowflake" and lightly pencil the numbers one through four on each part. (See Figure 5-72B.) Repeat this numbering sequence on the main body of the valentine. When the numbering is complete, the white "snowflake" is cut apart on the folded lines.

6. "Snowflake" quadrants 4 & 2 are then pasted over the red triangles. Quadrants 1 & 3 are pasted to the 9 x 12″ paper directly behind the two red hearts. (See lead illustration.)

When your kids have finished, explain that the hearts have to be taught how to "work." If these hearts are carefully pulled out away from the background when the card is closed — and then rubbed hard — the hearts will "remember" and perform every time!

5-70A

5-70B

St. Patrick's Day

At some time in the now forgotten past, St. Patrick's Day must have had something to do with a feast in the honor of the patron saint of Ireland. Somewhere along the line, however, it appears that this whole celebration was hijacked by a bunch of little people who, reputedly, bury their gold at the end of the rainbow.

In order to save future generations from a lot of bewilderment, I think that the time is long overdue to call this crazy festival by its real name—St. Leprechaun's Day!

Pass the word.

5-71

5-72A

5-72B

lesson 21   **How to Make a
                Shamrock**

Since one cannot be a celebrant of a Leprechaun festival without some knowledge of shamrocks, here are two quick ways to re-create the national emblem of Leprechaun Land.

5-73A

5-73B

5-73C

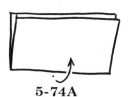

5-74A

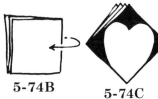

5-74B   5-74C

you need:

- for the drawn shamrock:
  pencil and paper
- for the cut-paper shamrock:
  a square of green paper, pencil, and scissors

to present:

The Drawn Shamrock. The shamrock is easy to draw. Simply draw three green hearts and add a green stem. (See Figures 5-73A, 5-73B and 5-73C.)

The Cut-Paper Shamrock.

1. The square paper is folded in half and then in half again. (See Figures 5-74A and 5-74B.) With the square turned so that the loose corners are to the far side of the paper, have your kids draw a heart as shown in Figure 5-74C.

2. When cutting out the folded heart, advise your class against cutting that part of the heart that falls on the folded edges seen in Figure 5-75A (otherwise the shamrock will fall apart). When the folded heart(s) is cut out, unfold the paper and trim away one of the green hearts to make a stem as in Figure 5-75B. Voila!

5-75A   5-75B

lesson 22   **Leprechauns**

Fashions in Leprechauns are always changing. In yesteryear they looked like fairies; today they have evolved into all kinds of fanciful creatures! Most of my Leprechauns resemble chin-whiskered Pilgrims and wear green Pilgrim-style hats with black hat bands and large white buckles. Here's how I do it:

For other *Leprechaun* suggestions see p. 234.

you need:

- practice paper
- 6 x 4½″ green construction paper
- 12 x 18″ drawing paper
- small rectangle of white "buckle" paper
- scissors, and paste or glue
- pencil and crayons (or other decorating materials)

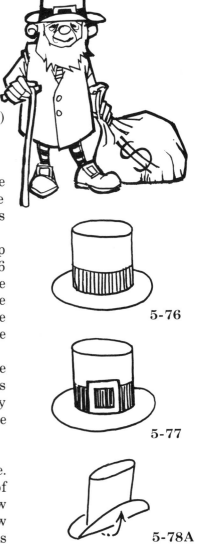

to present:

1. Have your kids practice drawing cylinders and the cake-on-the-plate concept as found on p. 173. The transition from a cake-on-a-plate to a Leprechaun hat is easy! (See Figure 5-76.)

2. Once your kids have practiced this hat on scrap paper, have them draw as large a hat as possible on the 6 x 4½″ green paper. The buckle is made by *cutting out* the center of the white paper or by *coloring in* the center of the white "buckle" paper with a black crayon. Paste the buckle to the hat band, and cut out the hat. (See Figure 5-77.)

5-76

3. Once the hats are cut out, have the kids turn up the brims, and paste the hats down on the drawing paper as in Figure 5-78A. Add the Leprechaun's head and body and proceed with the rest of the picture! (See Figure 5-78B.)

5-77

Further Sugestions: Kids love Leprechaun lore. The "I am told..." approach to the story about the pot of gold that the Leprechauns hide at the end of the rainbow will charm a whole classroom of children. Explain how the presence of Leprechauns in your neighborhood is considered to be a good omen, and that's why some people leave a bowl of milk outside their back door expect some of your young listeners to try it! A wonderful old story worth retelling is the one about the farmer who captures a Leprechaun, variously called *The Wise Leprechaun, Patrick O'Donnell and the Leprechaun, The Leprechaun and the Farmer*, etc. (see any book on Irish folklore). This story alone is worth the walk to the library!

5-78A

Alternate Lesson: With a change of color, this hat idea becomes a ready-made Pilgrim lesson!

5-78B

Easter

In the minds of most children, Easter's importance comes somewhere after Christmas, Halloween, and birthday parties, but considerably ahead of Columbus Day, New Year's, and *all* of our patriotic holidays. Rated on a one to ten scale, I would judge that it would get about a six!

Here are a few good ways to celebrate it.

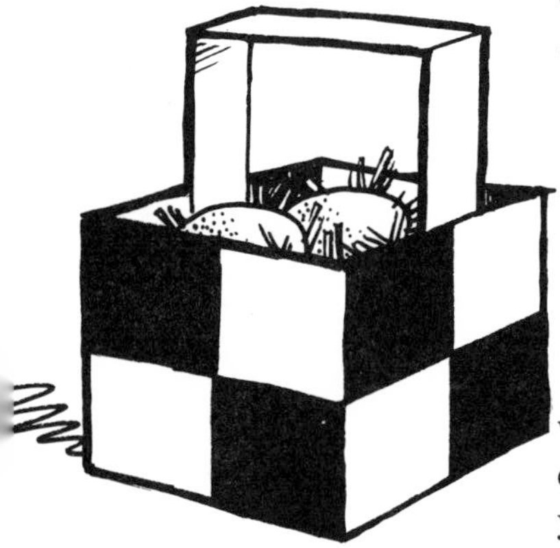

lesson 23   A Woven Easter Basket

Easter is a good time to introduce more weaving. This woven box is just large enough to hold a few pieces of candy and just small enough to set reasonable limits on your generosity.

you need:

- construction paper:
    - 12″ squares of assorted Easter colors
    - 6 x 9″ green
    - assorted scraps
- scissors, and paste or glue
- a bag of candy?

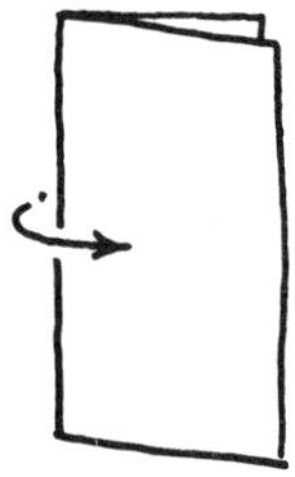

5-79A 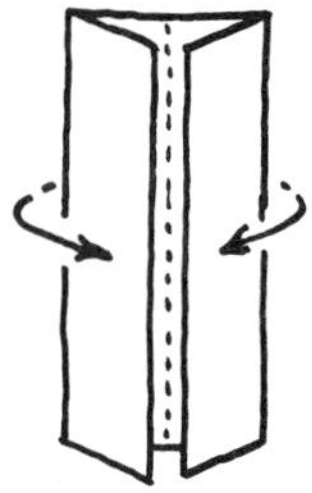   5-79B

to present:

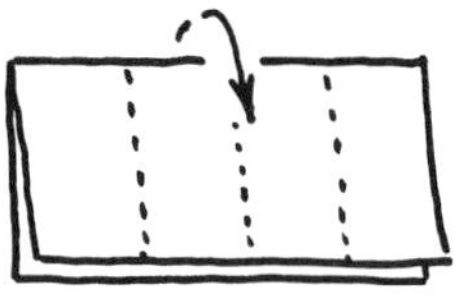

1. Have your kids fold the 12″ square in half, unfold, and then fold the sides to the middle. Repeat this series of folds from the opposite direction. (See Figures 5-79A, 5-79B, 5-79C and 5-79D.)

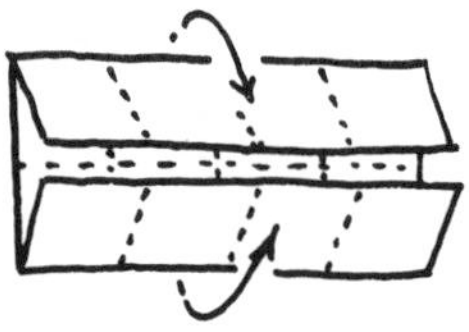

2. Once this Sixteen-Part Fold is complete, have your kids cut on the dark lines as shown in Figure 5-80.* Save all of the parts.

3. Remove (but save) the corners from the nine-part

5-79C

5-79D

---

*Once a very bright child asked my why I went to such lengths just to get a 9″ square divided into nine parts. The answer? All the cut-away parts are usable remainders. And besides that, have *you* ever tried to give ruler directions to a whole classroom full of kids?

square and cut on the heavy lines. (See Figures 5-81A and 5-81B.)

4. Once this point in the lesson has been reached, tell everyone to withhold the cross-shaped piece but to pick up all the *other* pieces that have been left over from the previous steps (the four-part strip, the three-part strip, and the four single squares), and to trade all of *these* pieces for all of *another* color held by a classmate. (In order for everyone to end up with a different color, some class members may have to trade more than one time.)

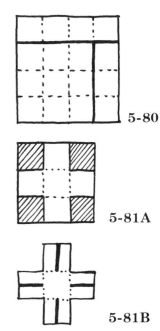

5-80

5-81A

5-81B

5. The four-part remainder strip is folded once lengthwise, and then cut on this new fold. (See Figure 5-82.)

6. One of the single squares is folded in half and cut on the fold as in Figure 5-83A. Each of these halves are folded once again widthwise as in Figure 5-83B. These small folded pieces are then used as corner braces or "joiners" to fasten the four-part strips into square enclosures (see arrows) as in Figure 5-83C.

5-82

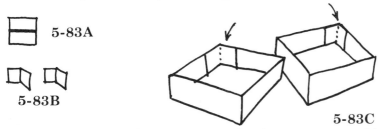

5-83A

5-83B

5-83C

7. Once the enclosures are made, the weaving itself is easy, just a simple two row in and out process. (See Figure 5-84.) When finished, have the kids paste down the ends of the upright strips.

8. The three-part strip cut in half lengthwise makes a handle which can then be pasted in place. (See Figure 5-85.) The green paper is used for "grass." Have the kids cut their green paper into long spaghetti-like strips, which can then be crinkled into a green excelsior.

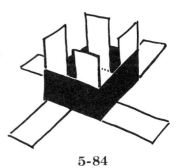

5-84

9. The remaining single squares can be added to the assorted scraps to be cut and decorated to look like Easter eggs. (Brown paper is always good for making chocolate bunnies, eggs, etc.; yellow paper is good for baby chicks, etc.)

10. And of course if you can add a few real candy treats to their baskets, this lesson becomes an instant celebration!

5-85

lesson 24

Paper Eggs (two styles)

you need:

- 9 x 12″ drawing and construction paper
- large egg patterns (see instructions below*)
- crayons (or other decorating materials)

*To Make the Egg Patterns. Here's one way using transparent or semi-transparent lightweight paper (tracing, writing, duplicating, etc.) and tag. Place the lightweight paper over the large egg shape that has been printed here, and trace it. Place the traced egg pencil-side down on top of the tag paper, and transfer this egg image to the tag by rubbing over the back of the drawing with the point of a pencil. Cut out one or more tag eggs for classroom patterns and begin!

Eggs Sunny Side Straight

This is the easier of the two approaches and can be used at all grade levels. Simply have your kids draw a series of vertical lines and decorate each section with a different design. (See Figure 5-86.)

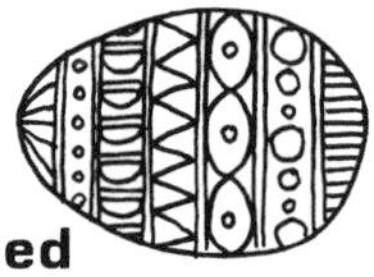

5-86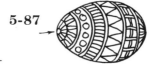

Eggs Sunny Side Curved

Begin by drawing a circle of any size (see arrow) at the smaller end of the egg, and then adding concentric arcs in the manner illustrated here in Figure 5-87.

5-87 →

For other *Easter* ideas see pp. 33 and 237.

Our Mothers and Fathers

Of the two parent-centered "holidays," Mother's Day is by far the most important. The reason for this is obvious: Mother's Day, in mid-May, has no neighboring holidays to interfere with its celebration. Father's Day, on the other hand, generally falls so close to the last day of school that it is lost in the *Grand Exodus!* Back-to-back with summer recess, even Christmas would have trouble getting a good billing this time of the year!

lesson 25   A Gift for Mother

This lesson combines a little bit of love with a little bit of acting ability to produce quite a lot of excitement. The subject may be placemats, but the total effect is pure childhood drama!

you need:

- construction paper:
     12 x 18″ colored + 9 x 6″
          same color
     9 x 6″ white (three each)
- pencil, scissors, paste or glue

to present:

Since many children may not know the difference between a placement and a doormat, the sooner you explain about placemats the better. Mother's Day placemats, naturally, are a *very special* kind of placemat, and that is what this lesson is all about.

1. Have your kids paste two of the 6 x 9″ white papers on the 12 x 18″ piece as shown in Figure 5-88.

2. After discussing with your class various ways of making decorative flowers (see Figure 5-89A) have them cut their 9 x 6″ colored paper in half widthwise and use each half for drawing and cutting out a flower decoration to be pasted in the center of each of the white areas. (See Figure 5-89B.)

3. Repeat the same procedure with the remaining 9 x

5-88

5-89A

5-89B

5-90

6″ white paper and paste white flowers in the center of each of the colored areas. (See Figure 5-90.)

4. NOW comes the drama. At this point in the presentation of this lesson I have the kids pause for a moment so that I can explain the *best* part!

First of all, I tell them, the big job is to get the placemat into the house without being seen. I usually put the placemat behind my back and go into a whistling and sidestepping "Hi Mom!" acting routine before I "hide" the placemat somewhere in the classroom in make-believe preparation for the coming Sunday.

Having instructed the class in the art of sneaking the gift into the house and hiding it in a safe place, I go into my early Sunday morning tiptoeing routine. I arrange to wake up before my mother, retrieve the placemat, and tiptoe to the breakfast table to set her place for breakfast using my special Mother's Day placemat. That done, I tiptoe away to await my mother's arrival.

Quickly switching roles to play the part of my mother ho-humming her way to the breakfast table, I am suddenly startled to see my special Mother's Day gift. I stop and with a questioning smile I say, "*Where* did this *nice* placemat come from?" And with that I slowly direct my gaze to encompass every child in the room (who by this time is absolutely radiant in anticipation of the coming event).

At that—I quickly revert to my previous role and state proudly, "*I* did it, Mother, I *made* it. Happy Mother's Day!"

Although this scenario may never qualify for an Academy Award, it has made a great many young children very happy. It has also made for many happy mothers!

Father's Day

Mothers are easy to please. They like flowers, birds, recipes, and all kinds of little, but impractical, gifts. Fathers, however, are less easily shoehorned into a standard stereotype. What will suit the beer and ballgame gang would be totally inappropriate for the tea and tennis set. So maybe it is just as well that Father's Day arrives at

the end of the school year where it can be gracefully
deleted from the classroom calendar for "lack of time."

But for those who need a Fathers Day lesson, here is
one lesson that is guaranteed to please *all* fathers.

lesson 26   **Big Daddys**

When it comes to cut paper, kids like to work BIG.
When the subject is Daddy, your children can take home a
giant-sized present!

you need:

- construction paper:
    - 6 x 9" trouser-colored
    - 6 x 9" shirt-colored (two each)
    - 6 x 4½" flesh-colored* (two each)
    - 4½ x 3" shoe-colored
    - assorted scraps as needed
- scissors, and paste or glue
- crayons (or other decorating materials)

to present:

1. The flesh-colored papers are to be used for the head
and for the hands. When drawing the head, be sure that
your kids include their father's neck.† (See Figures 5-91A
and 5-91B.)

2. The trouser paper is then folded lengthwise and
the class is instructed to cut on the fold for about three-
quarters of its length so that the resulting figure will
resemble a pair of trousers. (See Figure 5-92.)

3. The rest is easy. The trousers are pasted to one
sheet of shirt paper. The remaining sheet of shirt paper is
folded lengthwise and cut on the fold—these pieces will

5-91A   **5-91B**

---

*For a discussion of flesh-colored papers see p. 28.

†In order to provide for children who are fatherless, I find that it makes
sense to refer to this figure as, "Your father or any other 'big' man in your life."
This approach allows these children an opportunity to insert their own father-
figure such as a grandfather, an uncle, an older brother, etc.

5-92

5-93

become the sleeves. (See Figure 5-93.) The head and hands go just where you would expect them to go and the shoe paper is just large enough to make feet!

Patriotic Holidays

Due to the unpleasant aspects of war, Memorial Day, Veteran's Day, etc., do not loan themselves well to classroom creativity. However, here are lessons designed to channel creative energies into less bloodthirsty forms of art!

lesson 27   **Flag-Making**

Here are two ways to make flags—each is perfect in its own way!

The Basic Flag

you need:

• construction paper:
   9 x 12″ white
   4½ x 12″ red
   6 x 4½″ blue
• white chalk or white crayon
• scissors, and paste or glue

to present:

1. Have your class fold their red paper in half lengthwise and cut on the fold. Repeat this operation with each half to make four strips. Fold and cut each of these strips to make eight. (The pieces *could* be precut but this would take away part of the fun and much of the feeling of "doing it themselves.")

2. The first red stripe is pasted along the top edge. Leaving the white paper showing for the white stripes, the seven red stripes are pasted down. (See Figure 5-94A.)

5-94A

When the seventh is in position, have the kids cut away any remaining white. (See Figure 5-94B.) Their flags will now have thirteen stripes, seven red and six white.

3. Have your kids trim the blue paper so that it covers the top seven stripes (four red and three white) and paste into position. The stars can then be added with chalk or crayon as in Figure 5-94C. (For *Simple Stars*, see p. 46.)

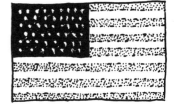

5-94B

5-94C

The Fluttering Flag

This advanced flag-making activity adds a real holiday touch to *any* picture!

you need:

- practice paper
- 6 x 4½″ white construction paper
- 9 x 12″ (or larger) manila drawing paper
- pencils, scissors, and paste or glue
- crayons (or other decorating materials)

to present:

1. Since the success of this lesson depends upon a number of procedural steps, the practice paper is just what you think it is for!

On the practice paper have your kids draw a wavy line as shown in Figure 5-95A. Although the vertical lines must be positioned exactly as shown in Figure 5-95B, their height is not critical at this point. After the seven red stripes have been drawn in the right hand section (adjust the vertical accordingly), repeat the stripe-making in the middle section. Only six stripes (three red and three white) are needed in the left hand section, the area above becoming the blue field. (See Figure 5-95C.) Note that each of these sections rises to a different height and that the blue field is the highest. Once the flag is understood, it is time to do a "good" one on the white construction paper.

5-95A

For another *Flag* lesson see p. 47.

5-95B

5-95C

5-96

2. Have your kids scratch out stars by using the point of their scissors against the crayoned blue field, and add the missing lines needed to draw the back of the flag. (See arrows in Figure 5-96.)

3. And finally, have your kids paste their flags on the manila paper and build a picture around it. The results will amaze you!

lesson 28   **Parade Hats**

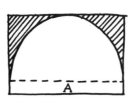

You don't need a holiday to enjoy these hats—they're good anytime!

you need:

- construction paper:
     6 x 24" parade colors
        (or 6 x 18" + 6 x 9" pasted to
        this approximate length)
     6 x 9" black
     6 x 4½" yellow
- stapler, and paste or glue

to present:

1. *Your* job is to custom fit and staple each long hat strip. (See Figure 5-97.) While you are doing the stapling, have your class working on step 2.

2. The hat brim is made from the 6 x 9" black paper. Have your kids begin by making fold A, a fold about 1" up from the bottom as shown in Figure 5-98. Unfold. Draw a curved line as shown and cut away the shaded areas.

3. The next line (indicate in Figure 5-99 by a dotted line) should also touch each end of the folded line. This line should be as smooth an arc as it is possible for the child to draw. This line is to be *scored*.

5-97

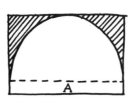

5-98   5-99

4. With fold A tucked inside the hat, staple the hat brim to the hat as indicated by the arrows. (See Figure 5-100A.) Then—*carefully*—fold the hat brim down on the scored line. (See Figure 5-100B.)

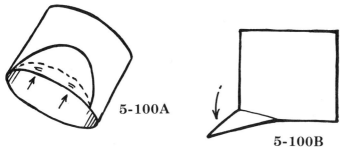

5-100A

5-100B

5. The upright plume is made by fringing the yellow paper, rolling it up, and stapling it to the top of the hat. (See lead illustration.)

Further Suggestions: This hat loans itself to all sorts of creative embellishments including insignias, visor straps, etc. Some of your kids will want to make a moustache from the leftover black scraps; others will want more yellow paper to make epaulets, etc.

For other hat ideas see pp. 174-176.

6

Stand-Ups

Many adults think of art in terms of pictures. Kids entertain no such delusions, for art is something you make — it can stand up or lie down or fly like a kite! The lessons in this chapter *stand up*, and by so doing take on a life of their own. Sculpturesque in approach, toy-like in form, these imaginative creations are just this side of the real thing! These things are *fun!*

lesson 1

Introduction to
Stand-Ups

Here are a few ways to make things stand up. Other ideas will be explained at length in the pages that follow.

you need:
- construction paper
- scissors

Slotted Stand-Ups

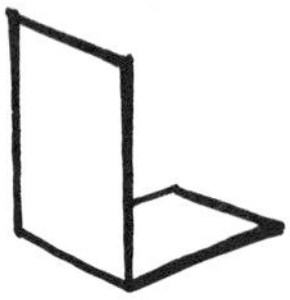

Horizontal Fold Stand-Ups

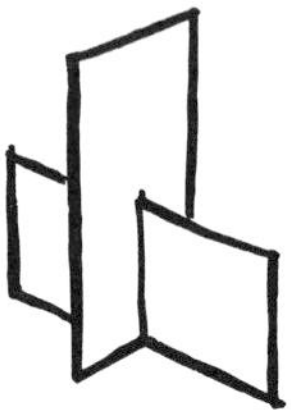

Vertical Fold Stand-Ups

Double-Fold Stand-Ups

Cut Flap Stand-Ups

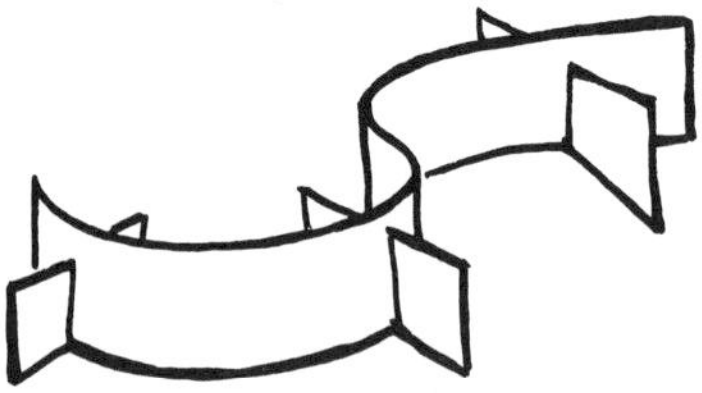

Slotted Centipede Stand-Ups

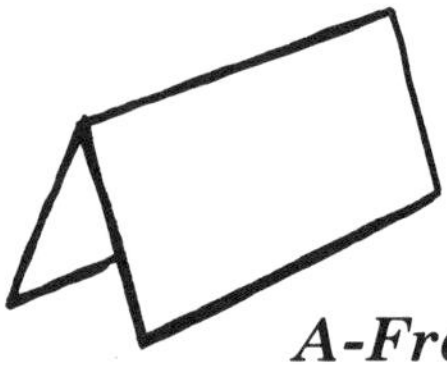

A-Frames

lesson 2 **The Roadside Stand**

Of all the lessons to be found in Part Two of this book (*Your Basic Bag of Tricks*), none is more useful than the Box Fold. Here it is again — this time as a roadside stand!

you need:

- 12 x 18″ drawing or construction paper
- odds and ends of scrap paper
- scissors, and paste or glue
- crayons (or other decorating materials)

to present:

1. Make a box according to the instructions found on p. 32 and then explain to your class that this box isn't a box — it's a roadside stand! Ask your kids to name some of the types of stands that they have seen — hot dog stands, cold drink stands, fruit and vegetable stands, etc. In short order you should have heard most everything from "ice cream" to "bait"!

2. To make the stands, have the kids cut an opening into the box as shown in Figure 6-1. (Be sure, however, to warn your class against having this opening touch any of the folds.) What your kids do from here on is their business — signs, shelves, counters, etc.

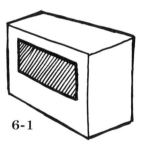

6-1

Further Suggestions: An even more elaborate stand can be made by making another box from a piece of paper just slightly smaller than the first. (See Figure 6-2.) This box will then fit inside so that the stand will have a back. This being the case, more shelves and the back door are optional.

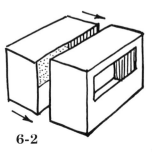

6-2

lesson 3   **Stand-Up for**
                Columbus

It may begin with a box fold, but it ends in a surprise!

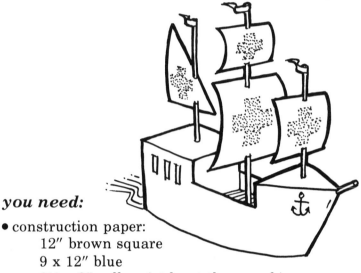

you need:

- construction paper:
    - 12″ brown square
    - 9 x 12″ blue
    - 2¼ x 3″ yellow (at least three each)
- drinking straws*
- 6 x 9″ tag for pattern
- scissors, and paste or glue
- crayons (or other decorating materials)
- stapler

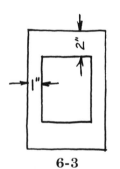

6-3

to present:

Preliminary Preparations: Although step 3 of this lesson can be managed without a tag pattern, a pattern would be helpful. See Figure 6-3 for pattern dimensions.

1. The 12″ square paper is to be folded into sixteen parts. Have your kids cut off one strip of four (as indicated in Figure 6-4 by the shaded area) and cut on the heavy lines.

2. Have your kids place a dot at halfway point A and draw straight lines A-B and A-C. (Crayon boxes make

6-4

*For instructions on making your own straws see p. 50.

good straightedges for short distances.) Score on these lines. (See Figure 6-5.)

3. Place the pattern on the brown paper as shown so that it is aligned with the vertical folded lines. Have your kids trace the inside of this frame pattern, and then lift it off to cut on the two longer lines—called here the X-Y lines — as shown in Figure 6-6.

4. The boat is now ready to be assembled. The stern folds up box style and is pasted, the middle section pushes inward to make a deck, and the bow is secured with a single staple and trimmed on the dotted line to give it a more rakish look. (See Figure 6-7.)

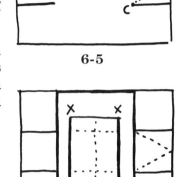

6-5

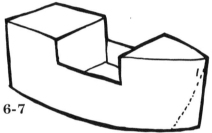

6-6

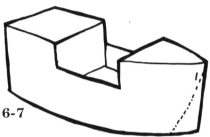

6-7

5. Very small holes are poked into the upper surface to provide for the mast, and the sails are added as shown in the lead illustration. (To provide a more solid footing for the masts, small pieces of clay will add that stability by anchoring the foot of the masts to the blue water paper.)

6. And that's it! All further embellishments are left to the artist!

lesson 4   **House Building**

Children love to see the world in miniature, and this house-making project is just their speed!

you need:

- construction paper:
    12 x 18″ house paper
    12 x 18″ grass paper
    10 x 7″ roof paper
    1 x 4″ chimney paper
    assorted scraps

   • scissors, and paste or glue
   • pencils and crayons (or other decorating materials)

to present:

   1. Fold the paper into sixteen parts. Remove the shaded areas and cut on all heavy lines. Place four lightly penciled X marks exactly as shown in Figure 6-8.

   2. Using Figure 6-9 as a guide, have your kids draw in whatever windows and door they want.

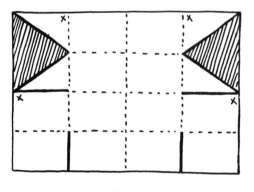

6-8

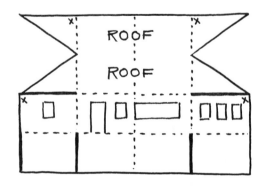

6-9

3. Fold up each house with the top flaps tucked inside in such a way as to bring the X marks into alignment. Paste. (See Figure 6-l0A.)

The roof paper is then folded lengthwise and pasted into position. (See Figure 6-10B.)

6-10A

6-10B

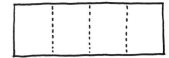

6-11A

4. To make a chimney from the red paper, fold it into four equal parts and using a scrap of red as a corner brace or "joiner" have your kids fold the paper into a box.* (See Figure 6-11A.) Cut away inverted V's on opposite sides of the chimney and place the completed chimney on the peak of the roof. (See Figure 6-11B.)

5. Place the houses on their own lots and ask your kids what they "need" to finish their housing development!

6-11B

lesson 5 **A-Frame Animals**

Although most lessons in this book loan themselves to one or two page developments, other multi-use ideas need much more room. To write down only the basic concept for A-Frame Animals would allow for some really good ideas to escape, so what you are about to see here is a basic animal body and a number of suggestions for putting it to use.

you need:

- animal-colored construction paper:
    9 x 12", 6 x 9", 6 x 4½", and 6" square
- tag strip 3 x 2"

---

*See use of "joiner" on p. 183, step 6.

- 3½″ (watercup size) circle pattern
- scissors, and paste or glue
- pencil and crayons (or other decorating materials)

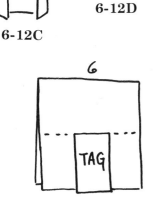

6-12A   **6-12B**

6-12C   **6-12D**

to present:

1. Have your kids fold the 9 x 12″ paper in half widthwise, open up and fold the short sides to the middle. (See Figures 6-12A and 6-12B.) Unfold. Fold about 1½ inches in on each of the long sides. (See Figure 6-12C.) Keeping these last folds in position, refold on the center fold. (See Figure 6-12D.)

2. With the paper still in its last position, have your kids center the tag patterns at the open end of the folded paper and trace each side (not top) of the pattern with a pencil as in Figure 6-13A. Cut on these two penciled lines through the folded packet. (See Figure 6-13B.) Overlap center tabs and paste. (See Figure 6-13C.)

6-13A

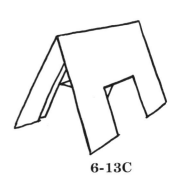

6-13B   **6-13C**

Basic Animal Head. Fold one of the 6 x 4½″ papers in half widthwise.* Keeping the fold to the upper right, sketch out basic head and neck as indicated in Figure 6-14A. (Be sure that the fold of the paper coincides with the back of the animal's neck.) Cut out through both sides of this folded paper and paste over the corner of the A-Frame body. Ears, horns, tail, etc., can be added as desired. (See Figure 6-14B.)

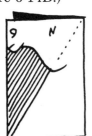 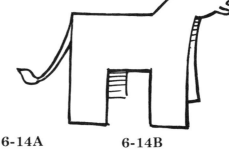

6-14A   6-14B

For a great Christmas reindeer, punch a hole at the top of the head and add a pipecleaner for horns. (Twist the pipe cleaner tightly to the top of the head and then double back on the remaining lengths to make antlers.)

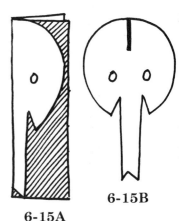

Elephant's Head. Fold one of the 6 x 9″ papers lengthwise and, with the fold to the left, draw in the head as indicated in Figure 6-15A. Cut away the shaded areas.

Open up and cut on dark line. (See Figure 6-15B.) Add eyes and Circlecone (see p. 38) top of head and paste. Curl trunk and add cut-paper ears.† The elephant's head can now be perched on the end of an A-Frame body where it will rest (and sway) easily! (See Figure 6-15C.)

6-15B

6-15A

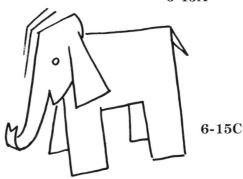

6-15C

---

*For giraffes and dinosaurs fold the 6 x 4½″ paper lengthwise.

†For a discussion on curling see p. 44.

6-16A

6-16B

Lion's Head. Center the circle pattern on one of the 6″ square papers. Draw a larger circle around the first. (See Figure 6-16A.) Cut out and fringe the larger circle as shown in Figure 6-16B. Draw in nose and eyes. Paste on cut paper ears and cut on both the long and short heavy lines. Circlecone top and bottom, and perch head on the end of A-Frame. Add tail and growl loudly! (See Figure 6-16C.)

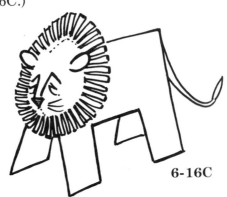

6-16C

lesson 6   **Toy Village**

In lesson 4 of this chapter I showed you one way to make a house. Here is another — completely different — approach to the same problem, and an apartment house thrown in to boot!

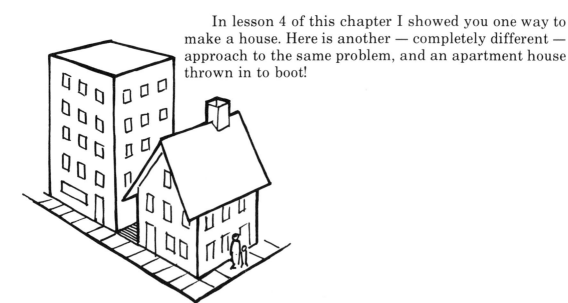

you need:

- construction paper:
    - 9 x 12″ house colors
    - 9 x 12″ roof colors
    - 5 x 1½″ chimney colors
    - 12 x 18″ building colors
    - 12 x 18″ ground colors
    - assorted odds and ends
- scissors, and paste or glue
- ruler or straightedge
- pencil and crayons (or other decorating materials)

6-17A

to present:

1. Fold the house paper in half widthwise and unfold. (See Figure 6-17A.) Find mid-point of front of house A and draw slope to each side of the roof (using ruler or straightedge). Draw line B-C of Figure 6-17B parallel to bottom of the paper. Cut on heavy line, and add windows and doors, etc., either with cut paper or crayons. If desired, doors can be cut so they open. (See Figure 6-17C.)

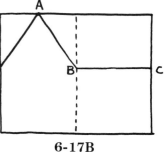

6-17B

2. Fold on all of the roof lines.* Overlap subroof to nearest roof tab and paste as shown in Figure 6-18A. Fold roof paper lengthwise and trim to allow for an acceptable overhang. Paste roof to subroof as in Figure 6-18B.

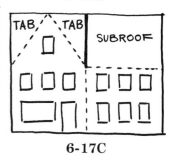

6-17C

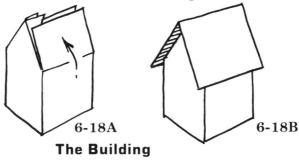

6-18A   6-18B

The Building

The building is relatively easy to make. Simply fold the building paper in half lengthwise and cut down the dark line a distance equal to one half the paper's width. (See Figure 6-19.) Add windows and doors. Overlap roof onto subroof and paste.

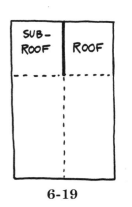

6-19

---

*The folding goes easier if the paper is *scored* first.

Stand-Up People

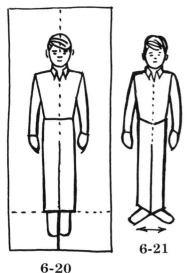

Have your kids draw their people legs together, standing on tiptoes. Fold lengthwise and cut out figure. (See Figure 6-20.) Do *not* cut between legs but fold at line of feet and cut up to separate shoes. The shoes are pasted directly to the ground paper. (See Figure 6-21.)

6-21

6-20

lesson 7   **Santa in the Chimney**

Here is the return of the Full-Paper Star (see p. 48), this time dressed in holiday red!

you need:

- construction paper
    - 9 x 12″ white
    - 3 x 18″ brick-colored
    - 1 x 18″ white
    - 9 x 6″ roof-colored
    - 6 x 4½″ black or brown
- pencil and white chalk
- scissors, and paste or glue
- crayons (or other decorating materials)

For another *Full-Paper Star* idea, see p. 49.

to present:

1. Have your class fold the 9 x 12″ white paper lengthwise, unfold, and draw a Full-Paper Star. Cut away the shaded portions indicated in Figure 6-22.

2. The kids can then begin to decorate the Santa Claus. (Trim under the sleeves for a better fitting costume.) Explain that since the lower half of the Santa will not be seen, coloring here is not important. (See Figure 6-23.)

3. The long white strip is pasted to one of the long edges of the red paper. A brick pattern can then be drawn on the red paper with the white chalk. (See Figure 6-24A.) When the brick pattern is complete, fold this long sheet into quarters and paste to make a triangular "chimney." (See Figure 6-24B.)

6-22

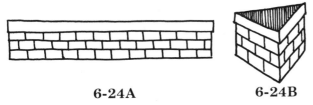

6-24A   6-24B

6-23

4. This Christmas centerpiece is now ready for assembly. With the Santa placed in the chimney and the chimney sitting on the roof paper — the holiday can begin!

lesson 8   Winter in the Country

In one form or another I have given this lesson dozens of times and each time it seems to be as fresh as the day I first introduced it. For a snowy day pastime, this lesson can't be beat!

you need:

- construction paper:
    12 x 18″ black
    12 x 18″ white
    3 x 4½″ white, red, and green

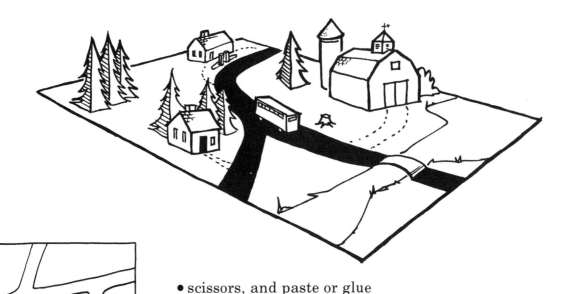

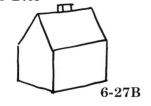

6-25

6-26

6-27A

6-27B

• scissors, and paste or glue
• pencils and crayons (or other decorating materials)

to present:

The Basic Landscape

1. Have your kids draw a few roads on one side of the white paper as suggested in Figure 6-25. Then scribble on the reverse side of this paper before cutting out the roadway. Save all parts.

2. The parts are to be reassembled on the black paper. (See Figure 6-26.) (The scribbled reverse side is to make reassembling easier.) Once this "puzzle" has been assembled, have your kids paste down only the nonroad or "snow" parts of the picture. When pasted, lift the roadway to reveal the basic winter scene.

The House. Draw the house on a 3 x 4½″ paper as shown in Figure 6-27A. Cut away the shaded areas, and score on the heavy lines. Fold the pasting tabs under, and fold back slightly on all scored lines to give the house an illusion of three-dimensions. (See Figure 6-27B.) Position and paste house onto snow scene.

The Barn. The barn is made in much the same way as the house except that there is one more roof line to score. (See Figures 6-28A and 6-28B.)

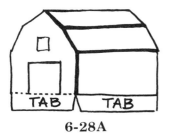

6-28A

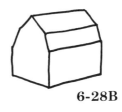

6-28B

6-28C

The silo (see Figure 6-28C) is nothing more than a paper cylinder topped with a Circlecone (see p. 38 for circlecone instructions).

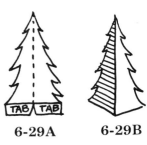

6-29A   6-29B

Evergreens. Trees of this type (see Figures 6-29A and 6-29B) are easily constructed using ideas found on p. 194. The tree shown here is a Double-Fold stand-up ("feet" in and pasted to the landscape).

Bridge. The bridge is the easiest of all. It is nothing more than a single piece of paper with two pasting flaps folded under. (See Figures 6-30A and 6-30B.)

Further Suggestions: Encourage your kids to add all kinds of details. If they need help getting some of their ideas to stand, review some of the basic stand-ups. Other excellent ideas are found elsewhere in this chapter.

6-30A

lesson 9   **A Bias for Stand-Ups**

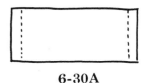

6-30B

In lesson 1 of this chapter I showed you seven different ways to make stand-ups. Here's another way that is less well-known and is perfect for making stand-ups sit!

you need:

- square pieces of construction paper
- scissors, and crayons (or other decorating materials)

to present:

1. This is one lesson where the illustrations speak better than words. The only thing to remember here is to

6-31A

6-31B

6-31C

explain to your kids that the greater part of the diagonal fold must remain intact or the figure will fall apart! (See Figures 6-31A, 6-31B and 6-31C.)

6-31D

lesson 10 **Creature Features**

Here is another way to make stand-ups. Your kids will delight in using this approach to make their wildest creatures come true!

you need:

- 9 x 12″ construction paper in assorted colors
- 9 x 12″ ground-colored paper
- scissors, and paste or glue
- crayons (or other decorating materials)

to present:

1. Have your kids fold their animal paper lengthwise as shown in Figure 6-32A. With the paper in this folded position, two or more lengthwise folds are made about ¾" in from each of the long sides. When unfolded, these last two folds leave creases indicated in Figure 6-32B.

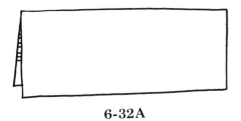

6-32A

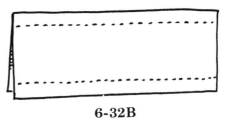

6-32B

2. The animal, whether it be fat, thin — or whatever —must follow certain very specific preliminary instructions. The back of the neck and the back of the body must coincide with the creased line nearest to the centerfold. The feet must touch the lower creased line. (See Figure 6-33.)

3. Four tabs are added as shown in Figure 6-34. One in the front, one in the back, and two for the feet. Have your kids cut out the animal through both sides of the folded paper and cut on all heavy lines. (Do not cut on the center fold.)

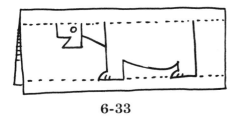

6-33

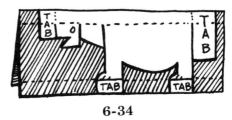

6-34

4. The head tabs fold in to close the front of the head, the rear end tabs perform a similar function at the rear of the animal. (See Figure 6-35.)

5. The pasting tabs are to be pasted to the grass paper and the head and neck are to be adjusted as desired. (See Figure 6-36.) For a downward movement of the neck, simply overlap the parts and paste; for upward movement use additional paper and paste to bridge gaps. (See Figures 6-37A and 6-37B.)

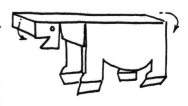

6-35

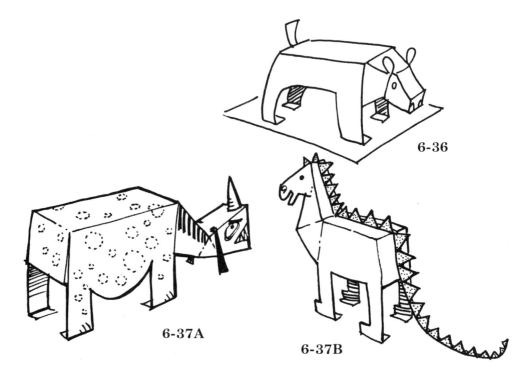

6-36

6-37A

6-37B

lesson 11   **To Frighten Miss Muffet Away**

Whether pinned to the wall, perched around the room, dangled on the end of a string, or carried off to the playground, these Circlecone creepie-crawlies are a childhood delight!

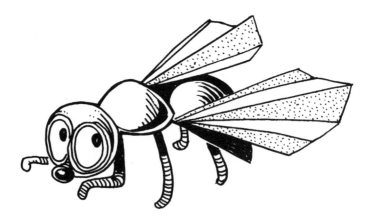

you need:

- construction paper in assorted colors and sizes
- circle patterns in assorted sizes
- paper straws (three each)
- tape, and string or thread
- pencil, scissors, paste or glue
- crayons (or other decorating materials)

to present:

Insect Legs

The legs of these insects are made by joining together the mid-section of three bent straws. For this, use tape, string, or thread. (See Figure 6-38.)

6-38

Basic Bug

Make the basic bug by drawing a face on a Circle-cone. The body is then balanced (or fastened with tape) on the legs. (See Figure 6-39.)

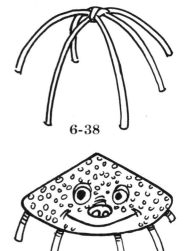

6-39

Two-Part Circlecone Bugs

A better Circlecone Bug is made using two slightly overlapping circles, one circle being larger than the other. (See Figure 6-40A.) Circlecone each end and continue as in the instructions given for the Basic Bug of the previous lesson. (See Figures 6-40B and 6-40C.)

6-40B

Three-Part Circlecone Bugs

6-40A

This, the best of all the Circlecone Bugs, is made by using three circles of diminishing sizes. (See Figure 6-41A.) Unlike the bugs explained earlier in this lesson, the positioning of the head circle is most important. (See Figure 6-41B.)

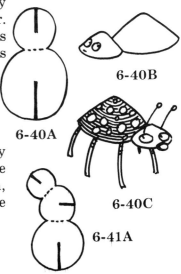

6-40C

6-41A

6-41B

For basic Circlecone instructions see p. 38

Wing Instructions: To make wings for the three-part Circlecone bug as illustrated in the lead figure:

1. Draw and cut out the wing shape as suggested in Figure 6-42. Make width A just wide enough to clear the insect's body.

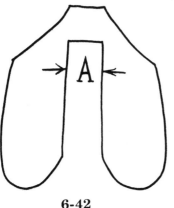

6-42

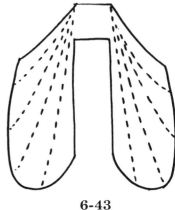

6-43

2. Score on the fan-shaped pattern of the dotted lines, and fold into pleat-like wings. (See Figure 6-43.)

Further Suggestions: Insects on long strings can be hung from the ceiling — bugs on short strings can be "taken for a walk"!

lesson 12

Perching Birds

These birds can be made by the flock. They are easy to make and as decorative as blossoms on a fruit tree!

you need:

- construction paper in assorted colors:
    3 x 4½″
    3 x 2¼″
- scrap paper
- scissors, and paste or glue
- pencil and crayons
- paper clips

to present:

1. Using one large and one small sheet of contrasting colors of construction paper, make Sailboat Cones*. (See Figures 6-44A and 6-44B.)

6-44A

6-44B

2. The larger of these two cones will become the top of the bird. Remove the shaded areas of this larger cone. (See Figure 6-45A.) Have your kids slit the tail before placing it over the end of the small cone. (See Figure 6-45B.)

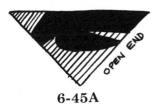

6-45A

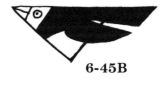

6-45B

3. Add eyes, beak, flare out wings, and stuff with scrap paper to fill out body (just a *small* ball of scrap paper will do). Using a paperclip, fasten the bird to any convenient perch!

---

*For Sailboat Cone instructions see p. 52.

7

Watch Closely-
Action Pictures !

As far as children are concerned, pictures that move are nothing less than a natural art form. If most kids had their way, *Mona Lisa* would wink and Michelangelo's *David* would squirt water!

Here then is an outrageous collection of lessons that do everything but draw themselves. Some of them wink, some talk, some roll their eyes — all are lots of fun. I call these things *ACTION PICTURES* and I give you my solemn guarantee that your kids will love them!

lesson 1 **Mouth and Eye Pictures**

Some lessons just happen—this was one of them. One Sunday afternoon the younger members of my family and I were sitting around the dining-room table "making things" when somebody cut a hole in a piece of paper, held it up to his mouth, and said something. The effect was so funny that immediately we all began to invent our own "mouth pictures." By Monday morning our Sunday pastime had become a polished art lesson. Here is how it goes.

you need:

- 9 x 12″ (or larger) drawing paper
- scissors
- crayons

to present:

Mouth Pictures

1. A Mouth Picture needs nothing more than a piece of paper with a hole cut out of it and a picture drawn around this "starter." The easiest way to get this lesson off the ground is for you to prepare a couple of samples ahead of time. Don't worry about your drawing — nobody's going to notice! (See Figures 7-1A, 7-1B and 7-1C.)

2. After the kids get the idea, suggest sideviews — they're just as funny! (See Figures 7-2A and 7-2B.)

7-1A

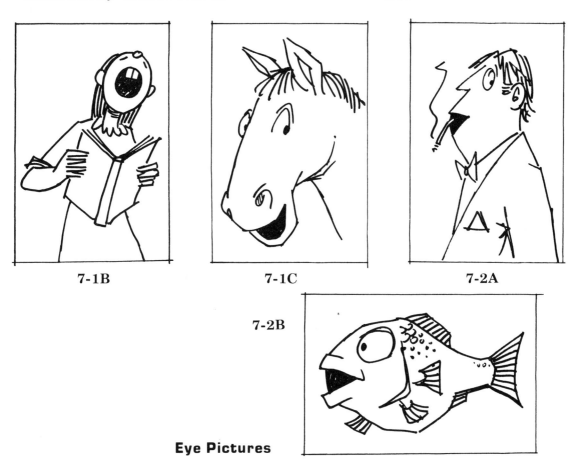

7-1B   7-1C   7-2A

7-2B

Eye Pictures

Eye pictures are done in the same way. Here are a couple of ideas to get you started (see Figures 7-3A and 7-3B):

7-3A

7-3B

lesson 2   **Roll-Ups**

If there is anything that excites children, it is the making of their own animated cartoons. This lesson is one of the best!

you need:

- 3 x 9″ paper
- 3 x 4½″ paper
- pencil

to present:

7-4A

1. Have your kids shade in the smaller paper with a pencil to make a "carbon" sheet as in Figure 7-4A. Fold the larger paper in half widthwise and insert the carbon sheet face down between the flaps. (See Figure 7-4B.)

2. Draw a simple cartoon on the front cover as in Figure 7-5A. Open up the top flap and remove the carbon to expose the lightly-transferred image. Using a pencil, make some major expression changes and then darken up the remaining transferred image as shown in Figure 7-5B.

7-4B

7-5A

7-5B

7-6A

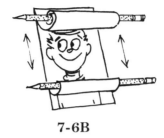

7-6B

3. Using their pencils as a curling tool, have your kids roll up the top sheet until it begins to act like a coiled spring. (See Figure 7-6A.) Although difficult to illustrate here, a simple back-and-forth movement will bring instant animation! (See Figure 7-6B.)

lesson 3   ## Halloween Flip-Faces

It never ceases to amaze me as to the amount of fun that kids can find in a simple flap, but here is another lesson that never fails to delight!

you need:

- 6 x 9″ and 12 x 18″ drawing paper
- 3½″ (watercup size) circle patterns
- pencils, scissors, and paste
- crayons

to present:

1. Have your kids trace two circles on the 9 x 6″ paper. Have them draw and color their own frontview face on one of the circles as shown in Figure 7-7. (Explain that ears or hair that extend beyond the limits of the circle will be added later.) Cut out both this face and the blank circle.

2. The head is to be folded in half horizontally and the bottom half is then pasted to the lower half of the blank circle. (See Figure 7-8A.) Fold down the top half — this new blank surface is to be used for the Halloween mask. Have your kids decorate these in their own way. (See Figure 7-8B.)

7-7

Once the mask is done, the backside of the Flip-Face is pasted to the top of the drawing paper as in lead illustration on previous page.(Ears and hair can now be added.) And finally — add in the rest of the costume!

7-8A

lesson 4   **Flip-Flops**

The idea of changing images by superimposition must be as old as picture making and as new as the day that your class suddenly discovers Flip-Flops and their fun making possibilities!

you need:

7-8B

- 12 x 18″ drawing paper
- scissors
- crayons

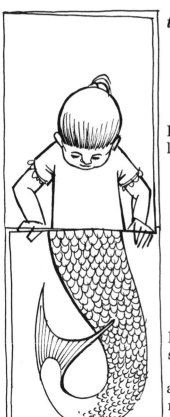

to present:

People Flip-Flops

1. The papers are folded into eight parts as shown in Figure 7-9. Remove shaded areas and cut on the heavy lines.

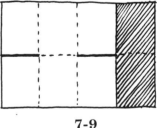

7-9

2. Have your kids draw a figure in the center section. Be sure to explain that, for best results, the waistline should fall on the horizontal fold. (See Figure 7-10.)

3. The rest is easy to figure out. Add changes one flap at a time. Turn girls into boys, boys into monsters, monsters into robots, etc.! (See Figure 7-11.)

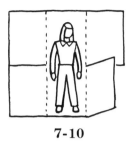

7-10

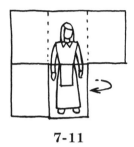

7-11

Animal Flip-Flops

1. Begin as in People Flip-Flops but this time turn the paper vertically rather than horizontally. (See Figures 7-12A, 7-12B and 7-12C.) Animals can change into other animals, into birds, beasts, insects, etc. (Boys, in particular, will delight in turning animals into automobiles, etc.!)

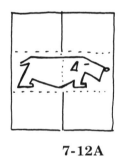

7-12A

7-12B

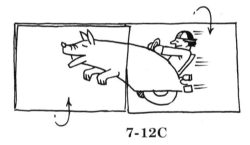

7-12C

lesson 5   **Moving Eyes**

Here is another natural for children. It's nothing more than a few holes cut in a piece of paper and yet — kids really get excited over this one!

you need:

- 12 x 18″ prepared drawing paper (see step 1)
- 12 x 18″ unprepared drawing paper
- single-edged razor blades
- crayons

to present:

1. This lesson takes some prior preparation on *your* part for it needs paper with precut eyeholes. Using a single-edged razor blade (or any other sharp cutting blade) cut one or more sets of eyeholes in each sheet of drawing paper. (If your blade is sharp, you can cut through quite a few sheets at one time.) Don't worry as to the exact size and shape of these holes — if the kids don't like them, they'll change them! (See Figure 7-13.)

2. The actual presentation of the activity is simplicity itself.* All your class needs to get started is to know that these are eyeholes and that it's their job to "finish" the picture. A few prepared examples will help. (See Figure 7-14.)

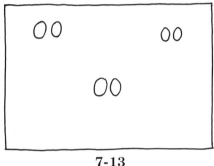

7-13

7-14

3. When the picture making is well underway, introduce the second (unprepared) sheet of drawing paper. This paper goes underneath the first. Pupils can now be drawn in the eyeholes as shown in Figure 7-15.

7-15

---

*In order to capture complete attention, I like to begin this lesson by holding up one of the prepared papers and apologizing for its condition. I explain that something "got into" the paper cabinet over the weekend and that we will have to make the best of it. By the time that the brighter members of the class begin to sense the put-on, the papers are distributed and I'm ready to begin.

Activating Instructions: To animate the eyes, simply move the papers slightly. Once your kids get the idea, prepare for immediate excitement!

lesson 6   **Ghosts!**

Ghosts are just as much a part of this culture as apple pie and ice cream. The mere mention of a *ghost* will make kids sit up and take notice. And to start a lesson with the promise of ghosts to come is excitement itself!

you need:

- 12 x 18″ and 6 x 9″ drawing paper
- black crayon
- scissors and paste

to present:

1. This lesson is best presented with prior preparation. Draw a street scene in black crayon (line only). Draw and cut out a few simple ghosts and paste them to the back of this drawing. Put the drawing to one side for step 3.

2. Begin your classroom presentation by announcing that "later on in the period we will be visited by ghosts, but right now there are other things to talk about." Turn the discussion to houses and buildings by drawing a rectangle and a simple house shape on the chalkboard. Have the kids come forward one at a time to add details. Explain that some of the most interesting drawings are often nothing more than the drawings with the most remembered details. Once this illustrated discussion has reached its peak, have your kids draw a street scene using black crayon (line only).

3. Once the street scenes are well underway, bring out your prepared street scene and, standing next to one of the classroom windows, call everyone's attention to your picture. "Watch!" you announce with a quaver to your voice. While all eyes are glued to your picture, make a high-pitched humming sound (a la TV mystery film soundtrack) and pull your picture slowly into the light. As soon as the ghosts appear, quickly make them disappear. (See Figure 7-16.) Repeat this move again for your delighted audience and you have made their day. Pass out the 6 x 9″ paper and let them make their own ghosts. *Your* work is done!

7-16

lesson 7   **Magic Eyes**

These eyes actually appear to *move!* Right, left, up or down, they follow your every movement. Based upon as clever an optical illusion as you will ever see, this blue-ribbon mixture of art and magic makes for an inspired Halloween lesson plan!

you need:

- teacher preparation materials:
    - 9 x 12″ dark-colored construction paper
    - 9 x 12″ white construction paper
- classroom materials:
    - 9 x 12″ manila paper
    - 9 x 12″ blue-green construction paper*
    - 6 x 4½″ (or larger) white paper
- scissors and paste
- crayons

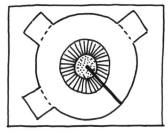

7-17A

to present:

Teacher Preparation: To best present this lesson you should prepare ahead of time a Magic Eye of exhibition size. From the 9 x 12″ sheet of white paper cut out a large circle with three attached pasting tabs and a radius line as shown in Figure 7-17A. Cut on this radius line and add a large iris and pupil. Fold up and paste Circlecone style with the "eyeball" inside the cupped Circlecone. (See Figure 7-17B.)

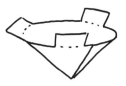

7-17B

Draw a blank eye on the 9 x 12″ dark-colored paper. This blank eye should be slightly smaller in its longest dimension than the width of the Circleconed eyeball. (See Figure 7-18A.) Cut out the interior of this eye. Place the Circleconed eyeball behind this opening and paste the two together using the eyeball pasting tabs. (See Figure 7-18B.) Once the two are together, hide this Magic Eye until it is needed (see step 2 below).

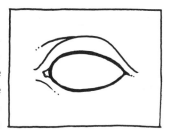

7-18A

Classroom Presentation

7-18B

1. Tell your class that they are to draw a mysterious picture in which the eyes are to play a key role. Explain that for reasons that will become evident later, the eyes cannot be too small and that the background will be added later in the period.

---

*Or any other not-too-dark "nighttime" paper.

2. Once this activity is well underway, introduce the large Magic Eye made earlier in this lesson. Pin or prop this eye in a prominent place and explain to your kids that wherever they may be sitting in the room, this eye is watching *them*. Furthermore, you explain, if they were to move, this eye would follow their every movement! Demonstrate this truth by having your class walk by the eye to experience its magic power. With that — send the charged up kids back to work!

3. Once the pictures have been drawn, have your kids cut out both the picture and the eyes to the picture. This picture is then pasted onto the blue-green paper. The background is added at this time. Once pasted, the eyes are then cut out through the blue-green paper.

4. And finally — the eyes are drawn on the small pieces of white paper as explained in the instructions given earlier in this lesson (see *Teacher Preparation*) and pasted into position.

Comments: Although the instructions may seem long, this lesson is worth every bit of time and effort that goes into it!

lesson 8 **Pilgrim Flip-Faces**

Earlier in this chapter I used a Halloween theme to introduce you to the basic Flip-Face. This Pilgrim Flip-Face is an entirely different use of the same concept. But Halloween or Pilgrim-style, don't let my themes mislead you — Flip-Faces are good anytime!

you need:

- 12 x 18″ and 6 x 9″ drawing paper
- 3½″ (watercup size) circle pattern
- scissors, paste, and crayons

to present:

1. Using the circle patterns, have your kids trace two circles on the smaller paper. Use one of the circles to make a sideview head. (The nose, incidentally, is the only part of the head that is allowed to extend beyond the edge of

7-19

the circle. Cut out both this face and the blank circle. (See Figure 7-19.)

2. Fold the head in half vertically and paste the back half of the head to the blank circle as shown in Figure 7-20A. Flip this face-flap and complete the newly exposed blank circle with the same face looking in the other direction. (See Figure 7-20B.)

7-20A

3. Paste the back of this Flip-Face to the top of the larger paper and complete the Pilgrim picture!

lesson 9 **Light Pictures**

Sometimes all it takes to awaken the creative spirit of a classroom is to introduce a new way of looking at things. Light pictures — a lesson in painting with light — does just that. If your kids are anything like my kids, they will be *delighted* with this one!

7-20B

you need:

- 8½ x 11″ lightweight paper (duplicating paper will do fine)

- pencil, pen, black crayon or marker
- scissors

to present:

Flashlight Pictures

7-21

1. Flashlight pictures are easy to do. Fold the paper in half widthwise and make a black line drawing of someone using a flashlight. (See Figure 7-21.)
2. Cut out the light beam from the top flap and then complete the missing parts of the picture by drawing them on the lower exposed flap. (See Figures 7-22A and 7-22B.)

7-22A

7-22B

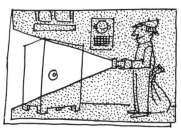

7-23

3. Hold the completed picture up to a bright light and watch the flashlight turn on! (See Figure 7-23.)

Other Light Pictures

Once your kids get the idea, they will be receptive to suggestions for other kinds of light pictures. A few more ideas are incorporated into Figures 7-24A, 7-24B, 7-24C and 7-24D!

7-24A

7-24B

7-24C

7-24D

lesson 10 **Shady Characters**

Old-fashioned hand shadows have always fascinated me but at best they are difficult to do and even more difficult to teach. And then one evening I suddenly realized that there was more than one way to make hand shadows — I call these wonderful creations Shady Characters!

you need:

- 9 x 12″ tag
- 12 x 18″ white paper
- pencils and scissors
- an opaque projector or any other strong light source

to present:

1. On the 9 x 12″ tag paper held horizontally, have your kids draw a large oval approximately 1½″ up from the bottom of the paper. Draw a vertical line to divide this oval in half. (See Figure 7-25.)

2. Approximately an inch to the left of the center line, another line is drawn parallel to the first. Divide this line in quarters. Draw line X-Y from lowest quarter mark as illustrated in Figure 7-26.

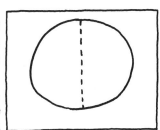

7-25

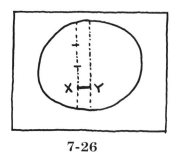

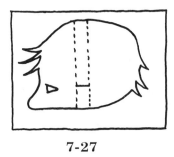

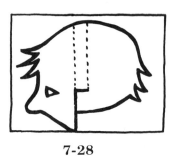

7-26   7-27   7-28

7-29

3. Straight across from the bottom of this oval head add a nose. Place an eye back from the bridge of the nose. (Note relationship of top of nose and placement of eye to the X-Y line drawn in step 2.) Add a suggestion of hair to the head. (See Figure 7-27.)

4 . Extend the lefthand vertical line to the bottom of the paper and draw a connecting line from the base of the nose to the lower end of this line as illustrated in Figure 7-28.

5. Cut out the eye, cut on all heavy lines, fold on all dotted lines. (See Figure 7-29.)

Operating Instructions: Although your kids will soon discover that there are many ways to hold these heads, begin by holding them as shown in Figure 7-30.

7-30

Now the fun begins! Have your kids hold these hand-operated heads up to a light source, and using the 12 x 18″ white paper as a shadow screen, begin your show. Different finger positions will produce a variety of different characters all funnier than the first. In seconds your kids will figure out how to make them talk!

Encourage your class to experiment by drawing their Shady Characters with hats, horns, teeth and any other details that will add to the fun.

Further Suggestgions: In Shady Characters you have enough material to keep your class busy for days! The shadows, incidentally, can be thrown directly onto a classroom wall. For a real professional finish, you might even have some of your kids construct a shadow theater from a cardboard box!

lesson 11   **Talking, Winking,
Peeking, Barking,
And Singing
Pictures**

This lesson is just as crazy as it sounds for it does everything it promises and more!

you need:

- 12 x 18″ drawing paper
- pencils, scissors, and crayons

to present:

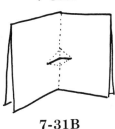

Talking Pictures

Have your kids fold their paper into four equal parts and then refold it lengthwise. Cut a "mouth" on the heavy line and fold on the accompanying dotted lines. (See Figure 7-31A.) The top half of the paper is then folded back as shown in Figure 7-31B. Using the full length of the cut as a "mouth" opening, have your kids complete the picture by drawing in an appropriate face.

Operating Instructions: Before the mouth will "talk," it has to be poked out from the rear so that the folds pop out as the paper is closed and retracts as the paper is opened. (See Figure 7-32.) Once the mouth has learned this trick, it will "talk" incessantly!

7-31A

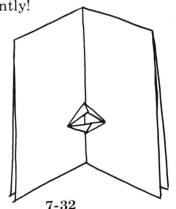

7-31B

7-32

Winking, Blinking, Peeking, Barking and Singing Pictures

Once the concept is understood, all kinds of things are possible, especially when your class begins to investigate double and offcenter folds. To illustrate some of the possibilities, here are a few suggestions (see Figures 7-33A, 7-33B, 7-33C and 7-33D):

7-33A

7-33B

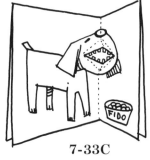

7-33C

7-33D

lesson 12   **Flip-Books**

If there is anything kids like better than watching cartoons it is making their own. Although Flip-Books are easy to make, good Flip-Book instructions are hard to come by. Here is the way that I do it:

you need:

- plenty of 3 x 2¼″ drawing paper*
- pencil and stapler

---

*The odd-sized 3 x 2½″ (1/16 of a 9 x 12″) is a size based purely on convenience and economy. If you are cutting up 9 x 12″ sheets to this size, figure on *at least* two per person (and don't be surprised if the demand exceeds this minimum estimate).

to present:

1. Give each child ten to twelve Flip-Book sheets. One of these small papers is to be shaded with a pencil so as to make a "carbon" sheet as in Figure 7-34. The others are to be neatly stacked.

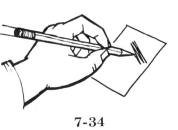

7-34

2. It is *your* job to do the stapling. With a bending motion, push the stack neatly and evenly to create the smoothly beveled surface of Figure 7-35A. Turn the stack over and place staple as shown in Figure 7-35B. Position stack as illustrated in Figure 7-35C with the two clamped ends of the staple uppermost. Have the kids place the carboned sheet (from step 1) face down under the top sheet of the flip-book and draw a cartoon with their pencils.

7-35A

3. When the cartoon is finished, the carbon is to be removed and placed under the next lower sheet. Small changes are then made in the lightly transferred image and then the rest of the image is penciled in exactly as it appears. (See Figure 7-36.)

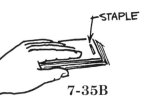

7-35B

4. This process with its transferred image and minute changes in details continues until the book is complete. When your kids riffle the top edge of their Flip-Books with their thumbs — their own animated cartoons spring to life! The possibilities here are endless. Prepare to be pestered in the days to come for "more books!"

7-35C

lesson 13 **Chatterboxes**

Later on in this chapter I will show you how to make box puppets, but this lesson on Chatterboxes achieves much of the same mileage in a very short time!

7-36

you need:

- three sizes of the same color construction paper:*
   9 x 12", 6 x 4½", and a 2" square
- 6 x 9" and 6 x 4½" hair colors
- 6 x 4½" white
- paste, pencils, scissors, and crayons

---

*Since this is a fantasy face, it is more fun if you prepare a selection of colors that include pinks, yellow-greens, etc.

to present:

1. The 9 x 12″ paper is folded into widthwise quarters as shown in Figure 7-37A. Unfold and then refold on the center fold as in Figure 7-37B. The kids are then to draw a mouth line from the center fold to the crease and to cut on this line. Open up and fold into the triangular shape shown in Figure 7-37C. Paste.

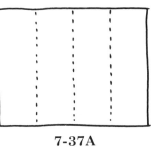
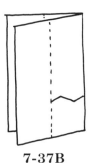
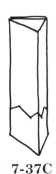

7-37A   **7-37B**   **7-37C**

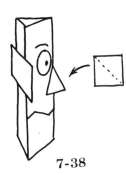

7-38

2. The 2″ square is folded diagonally to make a nose. The nose is pasted so that it overlaps the centerfold. The white paper is used to make eyes. The 6 x 4½″ piece of paper is large enough to make two ears which are pasted as shown in Figure 7-38.

3. Have your kids choose between the larger or the smaller pieces of "hair" paper. The "long hair" paper is folded lengthwise — the other, widthwise. The kids then cut away a face area, cut to make hair strands, and curl if desired. Paste when ready.

Eyebrows and other details can be added with either crayon or with cut paper. (See Figure 7-39.)

7-39

Operating Instructions: To make your Chatterbox "talk" is simply a matter of holding it as illustrated at the beginning of the lesson and waving the hand slightly to get the top half of the puppet's head to bob up and down. Once your kids get the knack, your puppet shows will begin!

lesson 14   **Lever Pictures**

There are many ways to make your classroom pictures come to life — but none are more popular than these lever pictures!

you need:

- 12 x 18″ and 6 x 4½″ drawing paper
- 1 x 6″ tag
- single-edged razor blade
- scrap of heavy cardboard
- large stapler
- pencils, scissors, and crayons

to present:

Simple Lever Pictures

Teacher Preparation: Using about half a dozen 12 x 18″ sheets at a time, staple them together as shown in Figure 7-40.* Then, using the cardboard to protect your working surface, cut out the stapled area. Repeat this process until you have enough square-holed papers to supply your class.

Presentation: Have your kids draw a large head on the smaller piece of drawing paper and cut it out. (See Figure 7-41A.) Position the tag lever as shown in Figure

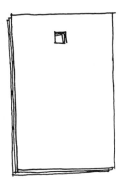

7-40

7-41A   7-41B

---

*For simplicity's sake, I am going to assume that you have access to a large desk stapler. If you plan to use a smaller stapler, reduce picture size to 9 x 12″ and shorten levers accordingly.

7-41B, center the business end of your stapler over the exposed part of the tag, and staple the head to the lever (see lead illustration). Complete the picture!

Advanced Lever Pictures

Once your kids understand this concept, great things can be done by letting them add as many moving parts as they can devise! (The only imposed limitation being that determined by the reach of the stapler.*)

The kids will draw their pictures and indicate in pencil those areas to be cut away: this *you* do with a single-edged razor blade.

Otherwise — proceed as before! (See Figure 7-42.)

7-42

---

*For advanced stapling techniques see section on *Punching, Cutting and Stapling*, p. 252.

lesson 15 **Giant Rabbits!**

Take my advice and don't give this lesson too early in
the day because this giant mask is one wild rabbit that is
guaranteed to disrupt all other school activities!

you need:

- construction paper:
     18 x 24″ white*
     6 x 18″ white (two each)
     12″ square orange
     4½ x 12″ green
- scrap paper
- stapler
- paste, pencils, scissors, and crayons

to present:

1. To begin the carrot, have your kids fold the orange
paper on the diagonal and twice again as shown in
Figures 7-43A, 7-43B and 7-43C.

7-43A

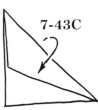

7-43B

7-43C

---

*Or two 12 x 18″ pieces pasted together to make one large sheet.

2. Fold once more, as shown in Figure 7-44A, to make a cone. Paste. Have your kids give volume to this carrot by stuffing the end with a wad of scrap paper. (See Figure 7-44B.)

3. The carrot top is made by making longitudinal cuts in the green paper as shown in Figure 7-45A. Roll or fold up this green carrot top and paste it inside the short end of the carrot cone. Once pasted, tuck in the long end-flap of the cone. (See Figure 7-45B.)

4. To make the rabbit mask, have your kids round one of the short ends of the large white paper and draw in a rabbit face. (The face that I have drawn in Figure 7-46 is easy to do. It is composed almost entirely of circles and curved lines.)

Cut a long ear from each of the 6 x 18″ white pieces. Color the inner ear pink and paste (or staple) the bottom only as shown so that each ear points inward. (See Figures 7-47A and 7-47B.)

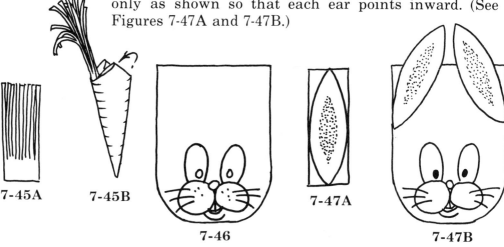

5. The top of the head is then A-Coned (see lead illustration). Since the rabbit's head is so enormous, the child sees through the large opening at the base of the mask.

And that's that — just stand back and let the rabbits take over!

lesson 16   **Box Puppets**

Making puppets from paper bags is such a time-honored classroom activity that I would be remiss if I didn't at least recommend bag puppets as a great classroom activity. Instructions for bag puppets can be found in many activity books — instructions for box puppets are less well-known. Here is how I make them.

you need:

- construction paper:
    - 12″ squares of assorted "face" colors*
    - 6 x 9″ assorted "hair" colors
    - 6 x 4½″ red
    - 1½ x 9″ white (two each)
    - 3 x 4½″ white
    - 9 x 6″ trouser or skirt colors
    - assorted scraps
- paste, pencils, scissors, and crayons

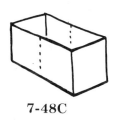

to present:

1. Using the Sixteen-Part Fold (see Figure 7-48A) have your kids fold the 12″ square and then cut off a four-part strip and save this strip for steps 2 & 3. (See Figure 7-48B.) Cut on the dark lines and fold into a box. Paste. (See Figure 7-48C.)

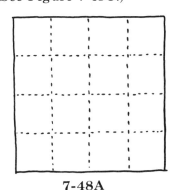

7-48A

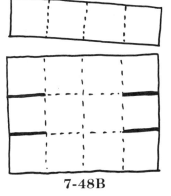

7-48B

7-48C

2. Cut on the two side creases as shown in Figure 7-49A. Taking the four-part strip saved from step 1, remove one square and save for step 3. (See Figure 7-49B.) The remaining three-part strip is pasted in place to become the top of the puppet's head.

7-49A

---

*Including green, etc.

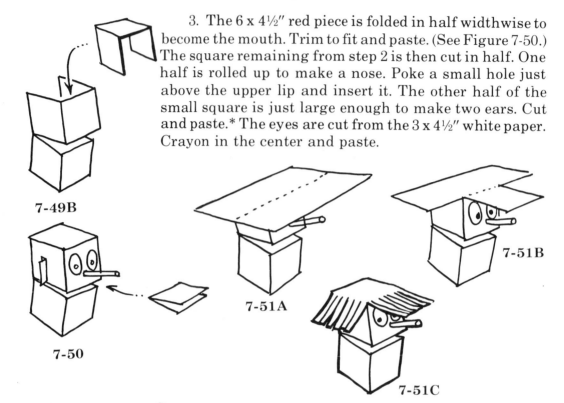

3. The 6 x 4½″ red piece is folded in half widthwise to become the mouth. Trim to fit and paste. (See Figure 7-50.) The square remaining from step 2 is then cut in half. One half is rolled up to make a nose. Poke a small hole just above the upper lip and insert it. The other half of the small square is just large enough to make two ears. Cut and paste.* The eyes are cut from the 3 x 4½″ white paper. Crayon in the center and paste.

7-49B

7-50

7-51A

7-51B

7-51C

7-52A

4. The hair can be made in a number of ways but perhaps the easiest is to fold the hair paper lengthwise, paste to the top of the head as shown, and cut, shape, curl, or fringe as desired. (See Figures 7-51A, 7-51B and 7-51C.)

5. Clothing can be made in a number of ways. Here are a few suggestions:

Shirt or Blouse. One of the long strips of white paper will become the shirt or blouse. Cut another in half to make sleeves. (See Figure 7-52A.) Add whatever pattern desired and then paste with folded ends of arms inside shirt or blouse as shown in Figure 7-52B. Paste this assembly to the bottom of the head.

7-52B

Trousers. Using one of the puppet's 3″ head squares as a guide, fold the 9″ length of trouser paper into thirds and paste, or staple, behind the head paper. Cut, as shown

---

*For one way to make ears see p. 150.

in Figure 7-53, to separate the legs and add feet from paper scraps.

Skirts. Fold and paste as for the trousers. Add legs and feet. (See Figure 7-54.)

No additional instructions are necessary, for your kids will probably take over with their own ideas long before you reach this point!

To Operate: Place the thumb in one of the head compartments and the fingers in the other as shown in Figure 7-55.

7-53

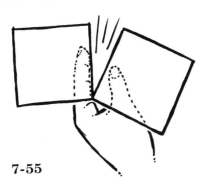

7-55

7-54

lesson 17 **Windballs**

In many ways this is the wildest lesson of them all. To begin with, you can't even do it until it's windy out, and I

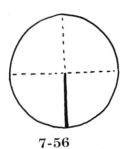

7-56

7-57

7-58

don't even recommend it at all if there is any danger of these Windballs being chased out into the streets. But if your play area is secure just turn these Windballs loose and chase them, race them, and watch them go!

you need:

- construction paper:
    6″ squares in assorted colors
- 6″ (shy) tag circle patterns
- paste or stapler (staplers preferred)

to present:

1. Have your kids trace the tag patterns onto the construction paper and cut out eight circles. Fold each of these circles into quarters and cut on the heavy line. (See Figure 7-56.)

2. These circles are then folded up and pasted or stapled into "air pockets." (See Figure 7-57.)

3. The air pockets are then assembled into complete spheres. When done — take them outside into the wind and let 'em go! (See Figure 7-58.)

lesson 18   My Favorite Airplane

I suppose that every boy grows up with a favorite paper airplane. This was mine — and I still think it's the best of them all!

you need:

- 8½ x 11″ lightweight paper*
- scissors

to present:

Here is another case where I feel that pictures speak better than words (see Figures 7-59A, 7-59B, 7-59C, 7-60A, 7-60B and 7-60C):

*Duplicating paper will do fine.

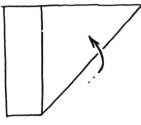

7-59A

7-59B

7-59C

7-60A

7-60B

7-60C

Optional Adjustments:

Wing Design

7-61A

7-61B

Flaps

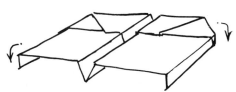

7-62A

7-62B

Tail

7-63A

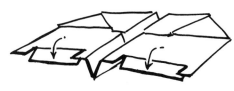

7-63B

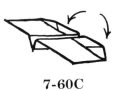

8

Addendum

No matter how well one tries to organize anything, there always seems to be a few things left over, things that are too important not to include and yet not important enough to warrant inclusion elsewhere. This is that kind of chapter and I think you'll enjoy it!

lesson 1 **Making Your Paper Cutter Cut**

Just because you know how to make a paper cutter cut, don't assume that this is the end of all knowledge. Although a masterful use of a paper cutter may not qualify as one of the Seven Lively Arts, a few selected tips from the experts will save you from a lot of unnecessary grief.

Choosing a Paper Cutter. The only important advice here is to choose a traditionally styled heavy-weight paper cutter such as the one pictured in Figure 8-1. My only reason for dwelling on this point is that every so often somebody invents another way to cut paper. Although some of these methods are extremely ingenious, I have yet to find an adequate substitute for the traditional board and shearing blade. For most class-room work, a paper cutter with an 18″ blade performs best! A paper cutter with a longer blade, while perfect for many things, takes up too much room, while a paper cutter with a smaller blade is just too small to be practical.

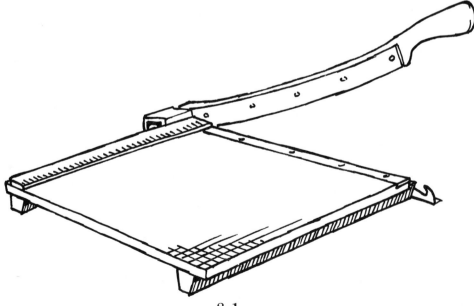

8-1

"What's Wrong with This Miserable Paper Cutter? It Won't Even Chop Through Twenty Sheets!" And after you have bought your paper cutter, hide it from the hackers. A good paper cutter is a piece of precision hardwear. Treat it with affection, think twice before loaning it, and keep it out of the hands of children. From a child's point of view, a ready-and-waiting paper cutter would tempt the devil himself, so if it is necessary to leave your paper cutter out (or if it is impossible to put it away), *turn it upside down when not in use.* This simple classroom precaution will save you a lot of grief.

Making Do. If your school has been in existence for any period of time, chances are that there are more paper cutters in the building than you might imagine. But most are has-beens. Like sins too large to bury but too embarrassing to be left in view, they're hidden away in back closets and on inaccessible shelves. Ask around, dig one out. Chances are that most of these paper cutters have been discarded simply because they are too *dull* to cut. So dust one off and take it to the local sharpening service. Usually the only important difference between a good paper cutter and a dull one is that one is sharp and the other needs sharpening! Pass the word along.

But in the Meantime What Do You Do? The most common complaint leveled against the community paper cutter is that it lacks the sensitivity to cut through *single* sheets of paper. The solution: until you get the blade sharpened, you'll have to feed your paper cutter in whatever multiples it cuts best. For this purpose keep some scraps on hand. (Last night's newspaper will do fine.)

What About Cutting Oversized Sheets? Given a sharp blade and paper stacked in the multiples that the paper cutter cuts best, anyone can give the illusion of proficiency. To become a real expert, however, you still have a few tricks to learn. (If you have ever seen somebody mangle a large sheet of paper or matboard in a small paper cutter, you know just what I'm talking about!) But first of all let me introduce you to your papercutter.

The "Style A" Paper Cutter

In order to determine whether your paper cutter is what I will call a "Style A" paper cutter, examine the end of the cutting arm. If it looks something like that depicted in the first illustration below, your paper cutter is definitely a member of the A family, and as such it has problems unique to its design.

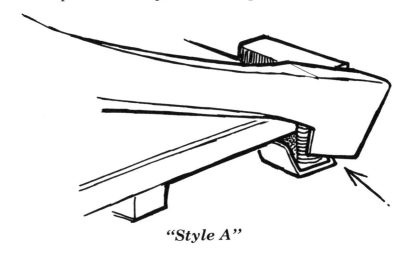

"Style A"

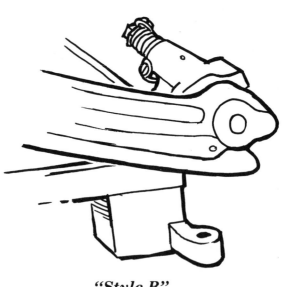

"Style B"

The problem is this: because of the placement of the spring housing, it becomes difficult to cut oversized sheets without damaging that part of the sheet that extends to the right of the blade. The damage comes quickly in the second cut, when the bludgeoning force of the spring housing clamps down to crush whatever paper or cardboard is in its path. (See Figure 8-2.)

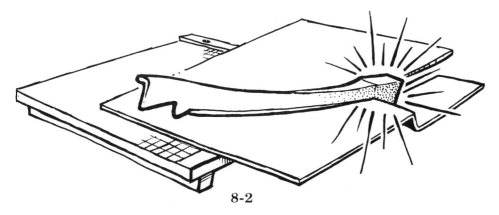

8-2

In areas such as art rooms where the paper cutter is in constant use, the problem can be solved through the use of a lowered offset shelf. By using a lowered shelf in this way, the paper or cardboard is allowed a safe and supported passage *under* the heavy end of the blade. (See Figure 8-3.)

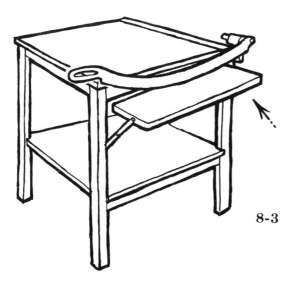

8-3

A makeshift shelf can be improvised by using two desks or tables of different heights. Using the lower table as the shelf, place the edge of the paper cutter on the edge of the higher table and cut. (See Figure 8-4.)

8-4

Large sheets of paper can be cut safely by simply separating two desks or tables (as shown in Figure 8-5)— so that the paper extending to the right of the blade can bend rather than break under the wrath of the descending blade.

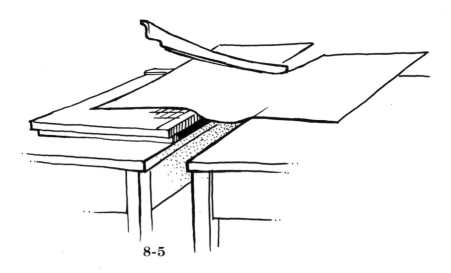

8-5

"Style A" and "Style B" Paper Cutters

But whether you have a "Style A" or a "Style B" paper cutter, both demand a lot of space. Furthermore, in normal operations, large sheets of paper or cardboard demand a great deal of additional space to the *rear* of the paper cutter. If your room is like my room, space is a real concern. Here's the answer:

1. Make the first cut in the usual way. (See Figure 8-6.)

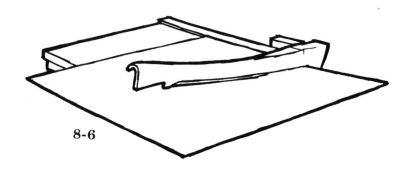

8-6

2. Then turn the sheet over so that the first cut aligns itself with the side of the cutting edge as shown here. Then cut again! (See Figure 8-7.)

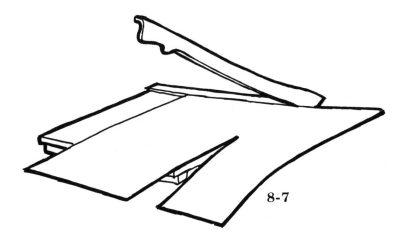

8-7

lesson 2 **Punching, Cutting, and Stapling**

Despite the fact that we live in a world dominated by high-powered printing presses, the search for practical knowledge continues to be just as elusive as ever. Given the millions of tons of printed matter that has been spewed out in my lifetime, the odds insist that somewhere in this world someone must have gathered together the same information as that appearing in this lesson. But if it does exist elsewhere — I never found it! It took simple experience to learn about paper punches, a lot of trial and error to learn how to cut paper efficiently, and a Branford, Connecticut shop teacher to explain to me the secrets of the stapler. Since all of this material was gathered the hard way, I consider this lesson on *Punching, Cutting, and Stapling* to be as valuable as any that this book has to offer.

Paper Punches

An expensive handheld punch will cost you over ten times the price of an inexpensive one, but for its limited use in art activities, a cheap punch will serve you just as well. There is one style, however, that comes equipped with a pelican-type bill to catch the punched-out paper. Since this feature adds little to the price while it keeps the floor free from dots, go out of your way to look for this model. And when you find it — buy it! (See Figure 8-8.)

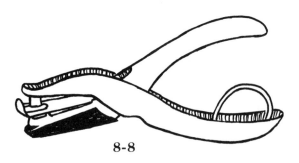

8-8

Cutting

Although many of the cutting problems are answered elsewhere in this book, here are a few more valuable suggestions:

When using your scissors to cut through a number of sheets of paper, staple the papers together. If your stapler is so equipped, use a temporary staple for this operation (see *pinning*, next page).

When using a sharp cutting tool like a hobby knife or a single-edged razor blade to cut through cardboard or stacked (and stapled) papers, take as many passes with the blade as you need. The applause here is saved for accuracy, so save your displays of strength for other areas of combat.

Stapling

For our purposes, let's reduce the list to stapling pliers, tacking staplers, and desk staplers:

Stapling Pliers. Stapling pliers bear a superficial resemblance to a handheld paper punch. For mobility it can't be beat, for you can wander around your room and staple as you go. What you gain in mobility, however, you lose in versatility. You cannot, for example, use stapling pliers to tack pictures onto your bulletin board. (See Figure 8-9.)

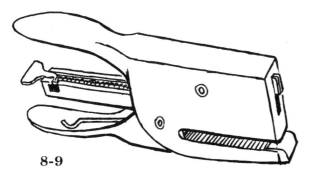

8-9

Tacking Staplers. For bulletin boards, nothing beats a good tacking stapler. But being another specialized tool, it is limited to just that — tacking! (See Figure 8-10.)

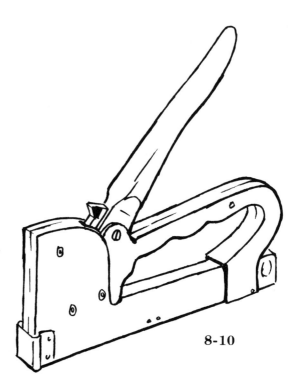

8-10

Desk Stapler. Although pliers and tacking staplers have their place, a desk stapler is everyone's first choice.* (See Figure 8-11.) A good desk stapler can tack as well as staple and (in some hands) can even be used in much the same way as the stapling pliers. By a "good stapler" I mean:

1. It should be large and sturdy with a 4" (±) stapling throat.

2. It should use standard staples. If at all possible stay away from staplers that use specialized staples. When you run out — you're stuck!

3. If you are buying your stapler through a catalog, the key words to look for are *staples, pins,* and *tacks.*

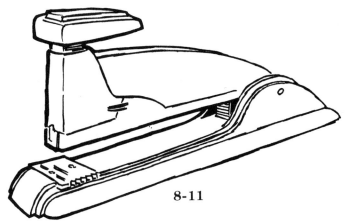

8-11

Stapling and tacking I think you understand. But pinning? What is *pinning?*

A stapler that *pins* is one that performs not one but two different clinching operations. The first is *stapling* in which the wire staple is clinched to look like this ⟋⟍. The other is *pinning* in which the clinched staple ends up looking like this ⌒⟍ The first is a permanent-type staple, a real fingernail tester if you have to remove it. The second is a temporary staple that can be easily removed — even by young children.

If your stapler pins, its anvil will be designed for both stapling and pinning operations. A typical anvil may look something like Figure 8-12.

8-12

The mechanics of switching from stapling to pinning differs from stapler to stapler. In some staplers it is done by pushing the anvil back a short distance; in others, the anvil is turned on its axis 180°. Either way, the mechanics of *using* the stapler remain the same.

More Stapling Tricks. To staple something onto the center of a large piece of cardboard or paper, place a couple of pieces of corrugated cardboard under the surface to be stapled, tack, lift up carefully, and clinch the ends of the staples by hand.

If you are stapling paper to heavy cardboard, try pushing two desks (or two books or tables, etc.) to within a very short gap of each other. Do your tacking over this gap. Then — lift up carefully and clinch the ends of the staples by hand.

If you are stapling paper to heavy cardboard, try pushing two desks (or two books or tables, etc.) to within a very short gap of each other. Do your tacking over this gap. Then—lift up carefuly and clinch the ends of the staples by hand.

lesson 6   **Putting Your Best Face Forward**

There are times when it's all the busy teacher can do just to *see* the pictures that the kids have made. There are other times when it's all one can do to get their pictures up on the wall. But there are also *special* times when an additional effort is called for, and for these special occasions your classroom pictures can be *mounted* or *matted*. If you are not already acquainted with the wonders that good mounting and matting can perform, then prepare yourself for a very pleasant surprise!

you need:

- paper or cardboard larger than the pictures to be displayed
- paste or glue
- tape, preferably masking tape
- pencil, steel-edged ruler, scissors
- single-edged razor blade or hobby knife

to present:

Mounts, Mats, and Cuffs

Mounting. To *mount* a picture is to affix it for display purposes to a larger sheet of paper or cardboard. For classroom use a picture can be mounted using paste, glue, rubber cement, or even a stapler. Although the mechanics of mounting are easy to learn, an attractive finished product demands more (as you will soon see) than the ability to use paper and paste.

Matting. To *mat* a picture is to display it through a window cut in a large piece of paper or cardboard. (See lead illustration.)

The simplest mats are made of paper. Although you can cut a pretty fair paper mat with scissors, a sharp single-edged razor blade held against a steel-edged ruler will do the best job.

Cardboard mats are by far the best but they are expensive and difficult to cut. Here a steel-edged ruler and a *very* sharp cutting edge are prerequisites. Do not try to cut through a cardboard mat with the first stroke of the blade. As long as the first cut is clean and accurate, you can use as many strokes as you wish. If you are cutting many mats, change blades often.

Oh yes — be sure that you have an old piece of cardboard under your mat-to-be or you may also be cutting a window into your working surface!

If your first attempts are less than perfect, you can often correct ragged edges with a piece of fine sandpaper.

Although masking tape is preferred for attaching a picture to the back of a mat, for classroom use one could just as easily use cellophane tape or even paste or glue.

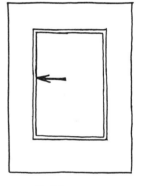

Cuffs. Sometimes a picture can be greatly enhanced by the use of a small inner mount or mat. This small inner border is called a *cuff* (see arrow in Figure 8-13). A mounted cuff is easy to make for it is just another piece of paper cut slightly larger than the picture. A matted cuff is an inner mat whose window is slightly smaller than the window of the outer mat.

8-13

Framing Theories

There are probably as many schools of thought here as there are framers, but all will agree that the background on which your picture is displayed should not detract from or in any way lead your eye away from the picture itself. After that note of harmony, the arguments begin. Here are capsule descriptions of the three schools of thought:

1. *The Traditional Method.* The traditional approach to framing is to frame everything in white or offwhite. Sometimes a pen line drawn around the picture will help to "contain the eye." (See Figure 8-14.)

2. *The High Contrast Approach.* Those who subscribe to the dark-against-light/light-against-dark school of framing often achieve dramatic results. The most obvious advantage to using this or the preceding approach is that you do not have to take *color* into consideration. (See Figures 8-15A and 8-15B.)

8-14   8-15A   8-15B

3. *Using Color.* And finally, there are those who feel very strongly that pictures in color should be framed using a colored background. (See Rule 3 below.)

Four Good Framing Rules

I know that many talented people can make up their own rules but if you are like most of us, you can learn a lot just by sticking close to some fairly stable guidelines.

1. The border surrounding a picture is normally of equal width on three sides but slightly larger at the bottom.

2. Smaller pictures look best against relatively large borders; larger pictures look best against smaller borders.

3. If you are framing with colored paper, select the color of your mount or mat from one of the predominate tones of the picture.

4. The color of the cuff is also chosen from one of the colors in the picture. Dark pictures often look good with a light or brightly colored cuff against a dark background; lighter pictures, a dark cuff against a light background. (For special effects — try using more than one cuff.)

Framing in a Hurry!

Here are some convenient paper sizes for quick and easy mounting:

• for 9 x 12" pictures use a 12 x 15" construction paper mount

• for 12 x 18″ pictures use an 18 x 24″ construction
paper mount

Here is an effective way of mounting pictures done on
8½ x 11″ duplicating or mimeograph paper:

• for 8½ x 11″ pictures use a 9 x 11½″ construction
paper cuff and a 12 x 14½″ mount

lesson 7   **Quick and Easy Displays**

The merit evaluation is coming up, the superin-
tendent is coming to visit, and the P.T.A. has chosen your
room for their next tea. What you need is a bottle of
aspirin and a quick and easy classroom display!

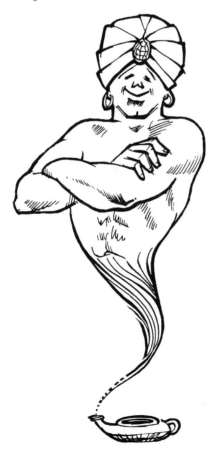

you need:

- plenty of paper
- stapler
- assorted clips and pins (more about this later)

to present:

Wall Displays. One of the first things a new teacher learns is that small loops of masking tape (or cellophane tape) will stick a picture to a wall. What they don't tell beginning teachers is that in some cases the removal of this tape also destroys the surface of the wall! The best advice here is to play it safe and check with the boss!

Bulletin Board Displays. There is a lot more to an attractive bulletin board than just covering it with a lot of pictures. The following rules should prove helpful:

1. In general, since most bulletin boards are dingy-brown and scarred from years of use, the most attractive displays are on bulletin boards which are covered with clean, crisp, construction paper.

2. *Before* you cover your bulletin board with paper, give a thought to your intended display. For example no matter how carefully you have cut your white mats, they are going to disappear against a bulletin board that has been covered with white paper!

3. Your best looking bulletin board displays are uncrowded in appearance. It is better to have just a few things attractively shown than to have dozens of things vying for attention.

4. Often the very nature of an art activity makes for a general overall similarity in picture color tones. If this is the case, you can frame all of the pictures alike; for example, all could be staple-mounted with the same dark cuff against a white border, or with a white cuff against a dark border. (For help here, refer to the framing rules in the preceding lesson.)

5. Since the most interesting bulletin boards are usually an exhibition of classroom work, make sure that the artists' names are clearly displayed. Seeing "who did it" is half the fun!

Suspended Displays. Hanging something from the ceiling is always an effective means of displaying three-dimensional work. The only advice needed here is to give some forethought to how your ceiling strings are eventually going to be removed. It is often a lot easier to get them up than to get them down!

"Clothesline" displays are another popular means of exhibiting art work. Paper clips threaded onto a string or wire work well as picture or project grippers. Spring clothespins work even better.

Chalkboard Displays. Pictures can be attached to chalkboard surfaces with loops or masking tape or fastened in place by *Quick Grip Clips.* (See Figure 8-16.) If you are not familiar with these clips, I suggest that you invest in a box. You'll find that they have many uses; a row of Quick Grip Clips will even support a mural! (For other means of display, you may find it profitable to browse through the *Clips, Pins, and Holders* section of any school supply catalog.)

8-16

Table or Display Case Displays. The rule here for attractive displays is the same for displaying anything else: keep it simple. Better to have a few things attractively displayed than to try to show too much. Use colored paper under your displays or, even better, use fabric. To add variety to the display, vary the exhibition level by draping the fabric over boxes of various sizes.

And Finally . . .

To reach the end of this book is like reaching the end of a school year — it is an occasion accompanied by mixed emotions. I can't say goodbye without reminding you again to use each lesson wisely, to present your material with warmth, to accompany it with humor, and to be the first to applaud the results. A good lesson is only a springboard — the rest is clearly up to you.

If you liked this book . . .

Tell someone about it!

INDEX